Declare His Glory
Congregational Worship Today

Declare His Glory

Congregational Worship Today

Editor
Harold Rowdon

With an Introduction by
Jonathan Lamb

Published for

by

paternoster
periodicals

British Library Cataloguing in Publication Data
A catalogue record for this book is available from the British Library

ISBN 0–900128–20–8

Cover design by Jordan Lance, Slough,
typeset by WestKey Ltd., Falmouth,
produced by Jeremy Mudditt Publishing Services, Carlisle,
and published for Partnership by
Paternoster Periodicals, P O Box 300, Carlisle, Cumbria, CA3 9AD.
Printed and bound in Great Britain by BPC Wheatons Ltd., Exeter, Devon.

Contents

Contents

Introduction

Of all the many activities in which our churches are engaged, it is worship which will last into eternity. The Songs of Heaven which are recorded in Revelation capture in vivid and imaginative language something of the powerful exuberance, the colourful dynamic and the rich texture of heavenly worship.

By comparison, our contemporary definitions and experience of worship seem painfully superficial and extraordinarily narrow. Whilst worship is high on the agenda at the popular level in today's evangelicalism, it is still generally very restricted in its scope. It is often to do with the contemporary music scene – the growth of worship albums, the flood of new songbooks with their OHP and CD-rom accessories, and the high profile worship leaders who now displace the Bible teachers on the publicity for our conferences.

In more conservative circles, some of our churches continue to struggle with a form and style of worship which we know can be equally restrictive and entirely predictable. Across the evangelical spectrum, we are aware of how pale our worship has become in comparison with the experience which awaits us in heaven, with its charged excitement and profound mystery.

It is therefore a particular pleasure to introduce this volume. Everywhere I travel I meet Christians who are looking for this sort of material. They are disturbed by the superficiality of so much in our evangelical sub-culture; they are looking for fresh ways of involving the whole community, young and old; they want to retain what is truly helpful from the past whilst responding to the realities of the twenty-first century culture in which they live; and they long for a spirituality with depth, which moves beyond particular forms and styles and, instead, expresses itself as an entire way of life rather than a specific event on a Sunday morning.

Declare His Glory helps us in this process. There is nothing else on the market which is so accessible in its style but which retains a depth of reflection and breadth of application. Each of the essays provokes us to consider new avenues of thought, and introduces suggestions for congregational worship which are full of spiritual insight and practical help. This is a book to expand our horizons and enrich our response at all kinds of levels. Whilst it is not intended to be a systematic treatment of worship, it addresses the subject from a variety of angles which readers are sure to find refreshing and stimulating.

The book is a welcome revision of an earlier title with the same name, published ten years ago, but which now contains important new material. In addition to the essays by John Baigent, John Allan and Peter Cousins, which were received so warmly in the first edition, Neil Summerton has reworked his essay, expanding it into two chapters and introducing some wonderfully helpful ideas in his proposed 'desirable reforms'. Then there are two new chapters by Alan Palmer and Eddie Prest which are very thought-provoking and are just what many of our churches need. I think these two contributions will ring bells with many of us – and our children and young people – and I hope that the proposals will be acted on widely.

It was said of the Puritan preacher, Richard Sibbes, 'heaven was in him before he was in heaven'. This collection of essays could help make that happen in our own lives and congregations – worship that begins to anticipate the joyful reality of our future home.

Jonathan Lamb

1

Worship: essence and form in scripture and today

John Baigent

*John Baigent retired early from a career in teaching, first as teacher,
then as trainer of teachers, in order to devote himself to Bible
teaching, not only in his own country, England, but also in
Scotland and other countries.*

INTRODUCTION

The purpose of this paper is to survey the main lines of biblical
teaching on worship and to consider how they apply to us today. It
begins with the widest possible definition of 'worship', noting the
different ways in which the word may be used, but eventually homes
in on the corporate worship of Christians.

No attempt has been made to provide an exhaustive list of biblical
references or to include more than a few quotations from modern
authors. Inevitably, there are aspects of the topic that could not be
covered in this relatively brief treatment.

THE ESSENCE OF WORSHIP

The meaning of worship

In English, the word 'worship' is both a noun and a verb. It derives
from the Old English word *weorthscipe* which meant the recognition
or ascription of worth. The two main ways in which the word is
used in English are: (a) to express and/or have feelings of adoration,
devotion, admiration, respect, etc, for things or people, but
especially for divine beings; (b) the formal expression of religious

1

adoration in individual and corporate acts, rites, words, services, etc.

Although the idea of 'worth' is not actually involved in any of the biblical *words* for worship, it is a thoroughly biblical *concept* to see worship as an acknowledgement of the worthiness of God (Rev 4:11; 5:12; cf Psa 29:2). Sometimes this idea is conveyed by the use of the word 'honour' (1 Sam 2:30; Isa 29:13; 43:20,23; Mark 7:6; John 5:23). It is also implied in 2 Samuel 22:4; 1 Chronicles 16:25; Psalms 18:3; 48:1; 96:4; 145:3, where the NIV translates 'worthy of praise' but the Hebrew simply reads 'to be praised'. (Similarly, in Deut 32:21; Psa 31:6; Jer 2:5 and many other places NIV translates 'worthless idols' where the Hebrew reads 'vanities' [lit 'breaths'].)

In the Bible, the verbs are basic. There are three main sets of Hebrew and Greek verbs which, in appropriate contexts, may be translated 'worship'.

To bow down

The Hebrew verb *hishtahawah* means to bow down, prostrate oneself, do homage, normally to God (Pss 95:6; 96:9; etc) or gods (Exod 20:5), but sometimes to a human being such as the king (1 Sam 24:8). These references show that other words for 'kneel', 'bow down' or 'prostrate oneself' are often used along with *hishtahawah*.

The corresponding Greek verb is *proskyneō* which also means to do obeisance to, prostrate oneself, reverence, and may (apparently) be directed to a human person (Matt 18:26; Rev 3:9)[1] or to idols and demonic beings (Rev 9:20; 13:4), but is normally reserved for the worship of Jesus (Matt 2:11; etc) or God (John 4:20f). Again, it is often associated with other verbs such as 'fall down'. (Some expositors make a great deal of the fact that *proskyneō* literally means 'kiss' or 'kiss towards'. It is true that its ancient pagan use would have been for stopping to kiss the earth or the image, but it is doubtful whether readers of the New Testament would have thought of 'kissing' when they read *proskyneō*.)

To serve

The Hebrew word *'abad* is used not only of a slave 'working' for his master (Deut 15:12) and an official 'serving' the king (2 Sam 16:19),

---

1. *Some would say that the NT uses proskyneō only in relation to a divine object, that* the king in Matt 18:26 stands for God and Rev 3:9 refers to the 'angel' of the church.

but of a worshipper 'serving' his god (2 Kings 10:18). Israel is called on to 'serve' the Lord and not other gods (Exod 23:2–25; Psa 100:2). In particular, the priests and Levites are 'servants' of the Lord as they 'stand' in his presence and lead the worship of God's people (Psa 134:1–2). However, the Old Testament normally uses other words, like *shārath* ('to minister') and *kāhan* ('act as priest'), when it describes the work of priests and Levites as they perform a variety of cultic actions (including offering sacrifices) in the sanctuary (Exod 28:1; 30:20; 1 Chron 16:4; 2 Chron 29:11).

There are two words in the Greek New Testament which correspond to the Hebrew words for 'serve', 'minister', etc. In non-biblical Greek *latreuō* meant 'to work for reward/wages'; in biblical Greek it normally means 'service to God', especially in priestly or cultic actions (Heb 8:5; 9:9,14; 10:2; 13:10), but also the worship or service of God or gods generally (Acts 24:14; 26:7; Rom 1:25; Heb 12:28; Rev 7:15; 22:3) and even worship in the heart (Rom 1:9). In classical Greek *leitourgeō* meant 'to do public work', but could also be used for performing priestly or cultic actions. This is its normal meaning in biblical Greek (Heb 10:11; cf 8:6; 9:21), but in the New Testament it is also used in a non-cultic way of various forms of worship or service (Acts 13:2; Rom 15:27; cf 2 Cor 9:12; Phil 2:17,25, 30).

To reverence

The Hebrew Bible contains a large number of verbs which convey the idea of 'fear' in its various forms, ranging from terror to awe and reverence which induce love or worship. The most common word is *yārē*. To 'fear' God is to reverence him in such a way that he is served not only in public and private worship (Psa 22:23,25; Mal 3:16) but also in obedience in everyday life (Deut 5:29; 13:4).

The New Testament uses the Greek verb for 'fear', *phobeō*, in much the same way as the Old Testament words are used (Luke 1:50; 18:2; Acts 9:31; 10:35). More specifically, it uses the verbs *sebomai* (lit 'to fall back before, shrink from') and *sebazomai* to describe the respect and reverence that is shown to God or the gods (Mark 7:7; Acts 19:27; Rom 1:25). The participle *sebomenoi* is used for Gentiles who took part in Jewish religious ritual, especially in the synagogue (Acts 13:43, 50; 16:14,17; 18:7). The noun *sebasma* is used of objects of worship (Acts 17:23; 2 Thess 2:4). These words are not normally used of Christian worship (but cf Acts 18:13). The word *eusebeia* referred to

3

'piety' (respect for relatives, judges, emperors, gods) but also to cultic worship (cf Acts 17:23). In the Pastorals and 2 Peter it denotes a way of life ('godliness') that arises from reverence for God (1 Tim 4:7–8; 6:3,11; 2 Pet 1:3,6f).

Two things need to be noticed here. First, most of the words we have looked at are not intrinsically 'religious' words: they can be used of actions and attitudes directed towards human beings (and even objects) as well as towards God or gods. Nevertheless, the Bible insists that 'worship' in its highest sense should be given only to God, for he is the only one who merits it (Exod 20:3ff; Deut 6:13; Matt 4:10; Acts 10:25f; Rev 19:10). (The fact that Jesus is also to be worshipped is a clear indication of his deity [John 5:23; Phil 2:9ff; Heb 1:6].)

Second, in the Bible, 'worship' usually refers to *outward* acts (kneeling, bowing, speaking, singing, performing ritual actions, obeying, etc), so much so that occasionally the outward acts *without any inward intention* are still described as 'worship' (Matt 20:20; Mark 7:7; 15:19). Nevertheless, it is normally assumed that the *external* actions correspond to, and express, *internal* attitudes and feelings (Isa 29:13; John 4:24; Rom 1:9; Eph 5:19).

To summarise so far: worship (in the Bible) means *to bow before God* (both outwardly and inwardly), acknowledging his worthiness and submitting to his will; *to serve God*, both in 'religious' or 'cultic' acts and in everyday obedience; and *to reverence God*, recognising his holiness and responding to it not only in special acts of 'piety' but also in a life of 'godliness'.

The scope of worship

We may distinguish three main uses of the word 'worship' in English. These, in turn, can be paralleled in the biblical usage of one or more of the basic words mentioned above.

Adoration

In its narrowest sense, 'worship' refers specifically to the adoration of God, addressed directly to God, telling him how wonderful he is and how much we appreciate him. In fact, it does not necessarily involve words; it can simply be the feelings of awe, wonder, love, praise and thankfulness which arise in response to the revelation of God. So Tozer defines worship as 'to feel in the heart and to express

4

in some appropriate manner a humbling but delightful sense of adoring awe and astonished wonder'.[1]

This kind of worship is well expressed in the words of a modern song:

> When I look into Your holiness,
> When I gaze into Your loveliness,
> When all things that surround
> Become shadows in the light of You;
> When I've found the joy of reaching Your heart,
> When my will becomes enthroned in Your love,
> When all things that surround
> Become shadows in the light of You:
> I worship You, I worship You.
> The reason I live is to worship You.[2]

In addition to the basic words, 'bow down' and 'kneel', this sense of worship is conveyed in the Bible by a wide range of words such as praise, bless, magnify, glorify, exalt, extol, rejoice in, thank, etc.

Obviously, distinctions can be made between some at least of these activities, but many of these words are used as synonyms in the psalms. Some commentators make a distinction between 'praise' and 'worship'. Praise is speaking well of God, recounting his attributes, telling what he has done (cf 1 Pet 2:9). It is an *outward* expression, addressed to others, whether believers or unbelievers. Worship, on the other hand, is the *inward* response of the heart, addressed directly to God (cf 1 Pet 2:5). This is a helpful distinction providing it is not pressed too far. Clearly some of our hymns and songs are *descriptive* or *ascriptive* praise (eg 'How good is the God we adore'; 'Jesus is Lord'), whereas others are *responsive* praise (eg 'Jesus, Thou joy of loving hearts'; 'Father, we love You, we worship and adore You'). But Ephesians 5:19 actually combines both aspects when it directs Christians to 'Speak *to one another* with psalms, hymns and spiritual songs. Sing and make music in your heart *to the Lord.*'

A careful analysis of the psalms suggests a distinction between *descriptive* praise (eg Psa 111), which praises God for who he is and

---

1. A W Tozer, *Worship: The Missing Jewel in the Evangelical Church*, Christian Publications, Camp Hill, Penn.
2. Author unknown.

what he has done in general, and *declarative* praise (eg Psa 34), which praises God for a specific experience of deliverance.[1]

Acts of worship

In this sense, 'worship' can be used to denote the public activities ('services') of a religious community gathered together in the presence of God and also the private religious exercises of a family or an individual. This wider sense of 'worship' will include not only ascriptions of adoration, praise, thanksgiving and blessing, but also supplication, intercession, confession, reading of scripture, teaching, prophecy, exhortation, words of knowledge or wisdom, testimony, speaking or singing in tongues, interpretation, healing, laying on of hands, baptism, the Lord's Supper, the collection and (even) the notices. It is *all* 'worship' because it is all done in honour of and in submission to God.

A number of recent writers[2] have queried whether this usage of 'worship' is entirely biblical. They would agree that the Old Testament words for 'worship', 'bow down' and 'serve', are used to describe both the work of the priests and Levites in the sanctuary and the response of the congregation (2 Chron 29:11,20–30) and that they included both the offering of sacrifices (Gen 22:3; 2 Kings 17:36; Psa 96:8, 9) and ascriptions of praise (2 Chron 29:30; Psa 95:1–2). But they question whether the New Testament justifies describing a Christian meeting as a 'service' or an 'act of worship'. Banks writes, 'Of course, in the New Testament the word "worship" is never applied to what Christians do when they meet together.'[3] And Marshall writes, 'To speak of a Christian meeting as being "a service of worship" with the implication that everything which takes place must somehow be related directly to this primary purpose is to depart seriously from the NT pattern.'[4]

Both writers are making valid points. Banks wants to emphasise that 'worship' should be a description of everything Christians do, not simply something they do 'in church' (see the next section, and the essay by Peter Cousins later in this volume). Marshall wants to

---

1. See C Westermann, *The Praise of God in the Psalms*, Epworth, 1966.
2. Eg R Banks, *Paul's Idea of Community; the Early House Churches in the Historical Setting*, Paternoster, 1980; R & J Banks, *The Home Church*, Lion, 1986; I H Marshall, 'How far did the early Christians *worship* God?', *Churchman*, 99.3 (1985), 216–229.
3. Banks, *Home Church*, 255.
4. Marshall, op cit, 226f.

stress that a Christian meeting involves much more than 'worship' (in the sense of addressing God); in particular it includes God addressing people and people ministering to one another.

All this is true. Nevertheless, the biblical concept of 'worship' as submission to God surely justifies our use of the word as a description of *everything* that goes on in a Christian 'service', providing it is all done for the *glory of* God and in *submission* to him, and providing it does not prevent us from using 'worship' in its narrower sense of 'adoration' and in its widest sense as the whole of a Christian's life and activity regarded as service to God. R P Martin tries to broaden the scope of congregational worship when he defines it as 'the dramatic celebration of God in his supreme worth in such a manner that his worthiness becomes the norm and inspiration of human living.'[1]

Total life-style

Ultimately, we cannot be satisfied with any use of the word 'worship' which confines it to particular times, places or activities. In its widest sense it must denote the whole life of the community, or of the individual, viewed as service to God, orientated towards God, submitted in obedience to his will, with everything being done to glorify him (1 Cor 10:31; Col 3:17).

In the Old Testament, the verb 'serve' is used with wider reference than simply performing cultic actions. In Deuteronomy 10:12f it takes its place as one of a number of synonyms (including 'fear') which describe the total response that God demanded from Israel: 'And now, O Israel, what does the LORD your God ask of you but to fear the LORD your God, to walk in all his ways, to love him, to serve the LORD your God with all your heart and with all your soul, and to observe the LORD's commands and decrees . . .?'

In the New Testament, this inclusive concept of 'worship' is very prominent. It is particularly denoted by the words *latreuō* ('serve as a priest'), *latreia* ('priestly service'), *leitourgeō* ('do priestly work'), *leitourgia* ('priestly work') and *thusia* ('sacrifice'), rather than by *proskyneō* ('bow down'). Paul saw not only his missionary work as priestly service (Rom 1:9; 15:16f), but the whole of his life (Acts 24:14). In addition to the continual 'sacrifices' of *praise* (Heb 13:15; 1 Pet 2:5), the Christian is called on to offer the 'sacrifices' of *acts of*

---

1. R P Martin, *The Worship of God*, Eerdmans, 1982, 4.

kindness and generosity (Heb 13:16; Phil 2:17; 4:18; cf Rom 15:27; 2 Cor 9:12; Phil 2:30). This total view of worship comes to its clearest expression in Romans 12:1 where the apostle appeals to Christians to 'offer your bodies as living sacrifices, holy and pleasing to God – which is your spiritual worship'.

The words of Gerard Manley Hopkins may have a Victorian flavour, but they epitomise this concept of worship:

> It is not only prayer that gives God glory but work. Smiting on an anvil, sawing a beam, whitewashing a wall, driving horses, sweeping, scouring, everything gives God some glory if being in his grace you do it as your duty. To go to communion worthily gives God great glory, but to take food in thankfulness and temperance gives God glory too. To lift up the hands in prayer gives God glory, but a man with a dung fork in his hand, a woman with a slop pail, give him glory too. He is so great that all things give him glory *if you mean they should* [my italics]. So then, my brethren, live!'[1]

And what is true for the individual Christian should also be true for the Christian community: everything a church does should be seen as its 'worship' to God. There is ultimately no distinction between 'worship' and 'service': all true service is a form of worship. That is how it will be for the people of God, both in heaven (Rev 7:15) and in the New Jerusalem (Rev 22:3).

The purpose of worship

For God

The primary purpose of worship (in all its various meanings) is to bring pleasure, satisfaction and delight to God (cf Num 28:2; Lev 1:9; Psa 149:4; Rom 12:1; Eph 5:19f; Phil 2:11; Heb 12:28; 13:16; 1 Pet 2:5).

God does not *need* our worship (cf Psa 50:9ff), but he *desires* it (John 4:23). This is recognized in modern songs like the following:

> I love You, Lord, and I lift my voice
> To worship You, O my soul rejoice.

---

1. Source not known.

Take joy, my King, in what You hear.
May it be a sweet, sweet sound in Your ear.[1]

Help us now to give You
Pleasure and delight
Heart and mind and will that say:
'I love You Lord'.[2]

The Bible does not *explicitly* answer the question, 'Why did God decide to create human beings?' or even, 'Why did God create anything at all?' What it does tell us is that everything God created derives from his will and exists to bring him pleasure and to serve his purposes (cf Rev 4:11). Thus the universe worships God by reflecting his glory (Psa 19:1; Isa 6:3; Rev 5:13). The angelic beings worship God by declaring his holiness (Isa 6:2–3; Rev 4:8) and carrying out his orders (1 Kings 22:19ff; Psa 103:20; Matt 26:53; Heb 1:14).

But the Bible *implies* that God was not satisfied just with the worship of the universe and the angels; he created human beings to stand in a unique relationship with him as his image (Gen 1:26f; Psa 8:5), to represent him and to serve his purposes on this earth (Gen 1:26, 28; Pss 8:6ff; 115:16). For the first human beings, this involved not only practical activities – tending the garden for God (Gen 2: 15) – but also times of intimate, personal communion with God (cf Gen 3:8f). Thus (as we saw earlier) everything a person does, can and should be an act of worship, in so far as it is done in obedience to God, out of love for him, to bring him glory and give him pleasure (cf 1 Cor 10:31; Col 3:17). Nevertheless, God desires, not simply our 'service-worship', but also a more deliberate and intimate form of fellowship in which we respond to him in words and actions which express our adoration of, devotion to, and dependence upon him (cf Gen 4:2ff).

God seeks not only the response of individuals but also the *united* worship of his people – all hearts beating as one in his presence (cf Rom 15:5f). He chose Israel to be a special people who would bring him particular pleasure and satisfaction (Exod 19:5–6; Deut 7:6; Jer 13:11) as they worshipped him in the way that he directed (cf Exod

---

1. Laurie Klein, Word Music [UK], 1978, 1980.
2. Graham Kendrick, Thank You Music, 1985.

25:8f), served him in an obedient life-style (cf Deut 6:1–5) and spread the knowledge of him throughout the world (cf Isa 42:1–7; 43:10,21).

God has brought the church into being (in both its total and local forms) in order to achieve the purpose that mankind as a whole and Israel as a nation have failed to fulfil (cf 1 Pet 2:9f). The church is now intended to be the sphere in which God receives the worship which his creatures owe him (cf Rom 15:6; 2 Cor 4:15; Eph 2: 12f; Jas 1:18) and the instrument through which he fulfils his purposes of grace and salvation for a fallen world (cf Matt 5:13–16; Acts 1:8; Eph 1: 10ff; 2:10; 3:10). Thus the church has both a priestly (1 Pet 2:5) and a prophetic (1 Pet 2:9) function. Everything it does should be done for God and for his glory (Eph 1:12), and this constitutes 'worship' (cf Rom 12:1; 15:16; Heb 13:16).

But it must also deliberately give time to occasions of corporate worship (Eph 5:19f; Heb 10:22; 12:28; 13:15) in which the overall orientation of the life and work of the church is focused and expressed. Corporate worship must, therefore, be given priority on the church's agenda because it answers to the desire of God's heart to receive his people's adoration and submission; not simply in isolated acts of individualized worship, but in a united response to him, like a polyphonic anthem from a vast choir, or a symphony from a large orchestra, with each member contributing a different but synchronized and harmonious part.

For human beings

When people worship, they fulfil the purpose for which they were created. As we have seen already, God has made us for worship; and if we do not worship God, we end up worshipping someone or something else (cf Rom 1:23,25). Worship is not only the *highest* occupation of human beings, in its widest sense it is the *only* occupation in which they should be engaged.

It is not surprising then that, when we worship God, we find it both a beneficial and an enjoyable experience. As we direct our attention to God and concentrate on him (rather than on ourselves and our own desires), our faith is strengthened, our motives are purified, our aspirations are lifted, our joy is increased; above all, the process of spiritual transformation is facilitated (2 Cor 3:18; cf Psa 135:18).

This is where William Temple's justly famous quotation fits:

Worship is the submission of all our nature to God. It is the quickening of conscience by his holiness; the nourishment of mind with his truth; the purifying of imagination by his beauty; the opening of the heart to his love; the surrender of will to his purpose – and all this gathered up in adoration, the most selfless emotion of which our nature is capable and therefore the chief remedy for that self-centredness which is our original sin and the source of all actual sin.[1]

And there is no need to restrict the beneficial effects of worship to the *spiritual* sphere. Consciously to put God at the centre of everything we do, say or think will bring not only spiritual benefits but *mental* and (even) *physical* well-being (cf Phil 4:6–7; 1 Thess 5:23). Worship has healing properties. Praise is positive: it lifts us above the difficulties and problems of life and banishes the negativism of discouragement, depression and despair.

So, when God asks us to worship him, he is not being selfish: he knows that worship is also for our good. As C S Lewis put it, 'In commanding us to worship him, God is inviting us to enjoy him.'[2] There is no need for us to be frightened of the word 'enjoyment' in connection with worship (cf Psa 147:1). Enjoyment can be 'spiritual' as well as 'carnal'. The famous words of the answer to the first question in *The Shorter Catechism*, 'Man's chief end is to glorify God, and to enjoy him for ever', apply not only to life in heaven in the future, but to life on earth now. There is something wrong when we do not enjoy worshipping God, when it is seen simply as a necessity or duty. On the other hand, there are dangers in *aiming* at enjoyment or 'thrills' in worship. Joy, like happiness, is a by-product which comes when we forget about ourselves and are absorbed in adoring and serving God.

For the church

Obviously, a church consists of individuals, and what has been said about the beneficial effects of worship on the individual applies to the members of a church when they meet together for worship. But there is also a corporate dimension to their worship. Worship builds up the church.

---

1. W Temple, *Readings in St John's Gospel*, Macmillan, 1939, 68.
2. C S Lewis, *Reflections on the Psalms*, Bles, 1958, ch IX.

When the Body of Christ meets consciously in the presence of God, all its activities constitute acts of worship because they are intended to glorify God. Thus worship includes not only the words and actions (and the thoughts and feelings) addressed directly to God, but also the words and actions communicated by God through the members of the body: in reading scripture, teaching, exhorting, prophesying, giving 'words of knowledge' and 'words of wisdom', speaking in tongues (interpreted), singing, laying on of hands, healing, etc (cf 1 Cor 12:7; 14:26; Eph 5:19; Col 3:16). In these ways, the time of worship not only brings pleasure to God but also strengthens the congregation (cf 1 Cor 14:3,12,26; 1Pet 4: 10f). In particular, the celebration of the Lord's Supper constitutes not only an act of worship but also a means of grace (cf 1 Cor 10:16; 11: 2–29).

The worship of the church constitutes a witness both to angelic beings (cf 1 Cor 11:10; Eph 3:10) and to unbelievers (cf 1 Cor 14:24f). In addition, praise and worship should play an important part in the spiritual warfare of the church. It is true that we have to go to the Old Testament for the clearest expressions of this function of praise (Psa 149:6–9; 2 Chron 20:21f). The classic treatment of spiritual warfare in the New Testament (Eph 6:1–18) speaks of 'prayer' rather than 'worship', but 'all kinds of prayer' (v 18) must include ascriptions of praise and worship.

If Satan 'trembles when he sees the weakest saint upon his knees', surely the confident praises of a group of Christians setting out to attack the strongholds of the evil one in evangelistic outreach are going to strike fear into the enemy! Such praise is not a psychological technique (people 'psyching themselves up' or 'singing to keep up their spirits'), but an expression of faith in a God who has already won the decisive battle and will give his people victory in each subsequent skirmish. The church needs to worship if it is to take the initiative in pushing back the frontiers of the kingdom of darkness. Praise is an essential weapon in the armoury of the Christian. This was well understood by the author of 'Onward, Christian Soldiers' (Sabine Baring-Gould) when he wrote:

At the name of Jesus,
Satan's host doth flee;
On then, Christian soldiers,
On to victory!

Hell's foundations quiver
At the shout of praise:
Brothers, lift your voices:
Loud your anthems raise.

Through worship the church is reminded that it exists solely for God's glory (Eph 1:12) and that it owes everything it is and has to the grace of God and the cross of Christ (Eph 1:3–8). Through worship, the church allows God to speak: to instruct, challenge, encourage, direct, rebuke, etc (cf Acts 13:1ff; Rom 15:4f; 1 Cor 14:26; 2 Tim 3:16). Through worship, the church remembers that it is the Body of Christ (1 Cor 10:17; cf 11:29) and that each member needs the contributions of the others (Rom 12:4–8; 1 Cor 12:7–11; Eph 4:7,11–16). Through worship the church is strengthened and equipped to go out into the world to serve the Lord in the power of the Spirit and to defeat the opposition (Acts 4:2–31; Rom 15:30, 16:20).

The bases of worship

The possibility of worship rests not with us, but with God. If God seeks worshippers, he must take the initiative and make worship possible. Three things are necessary.

The self-revelation of God

We could not worship God acceptably and appropriately unless he revealed his nature and his ways to us. You cannot really worship an 'unknown god' (cf Acts 17:23; John 4:22).

God graciously revealed his name (Exod. 3:15) and the character that that name signified (Exod. 34:6–7) to Israel through Moses, both in words and actions (Psa 103:7). Worship is, therefore, a response to the self- revelation of God: not simply to 'information' about God but to the self-disclosure of God encountered in the experience of his presence (cf Gen 28:1–17; 1 Kings 8:1–13; Pss 26:8; 27:4). As Donald Bloesch puts it: 'Worship is not a social get-together but a state of being grasped by the holy God.'[1]

The full and final revelation of God came in human form in the person of Jesus (John 1:18; 14:9; 17:6; Heb 1:1–3). He revealed the 'Father' not only by words but also by actions and character.

---

1. D G Bloesch, *Essentials of Evangelical Theology*, Harper & Row, 1982, 92.

Christians now worship 'the God and Father of our Lord Jesus Christ' (Eph 1:3; cf Luke 11:2; 1 Cor 8:6; Eph 3:14). But because Jesus is the divine Son of God, present in a special way when they meet together (Matt18:20), Christians also worship him (John 5:23; 20:28; Phil 2:9–11; Rev 5:8–14).

The work of Christ

As sinful people, we could not worship a holy God acceptably unless the barrier of our sins were removed. Only God could do that. So God gave his people, Israel, a sanctuary where they could approach him without infringing on his holiness and being consumed (Exod 25:8; Deut 4:24) and a system of sacrifices which 'atoned for' their sins and fitted them to live in covenant relationship with himself (Exod 24:5–8; Lev 17:11; Isa 6:5–7).

The once-for-all sacrifice of Jesus on the cross was both the counterpart and the basis of those Old Testament offerings (Rom 3:25; Heb 9:11–14; 10:5–14). The finished work of Christ is the basis of our acceptance before God (Rom 5:1–2; Eph 1:7; Heb 10: 19ff) and his continuing high priestly intercession is the basis of our assurance that we will never be refused entry into the presence of God (Rom 8:34; Heb 7:25; 9:24; 10:21), even though it is still true that 'our God is a consuming fire' (Heb 12:29). Jesus, then, is the mediator of a new covenant which enables Christians to join in with the incessant worship of the heavenly hosts (Heb 12:22–24).

The activity of the Holy Spirit

We could not worship God while we were spiritually 'dead' (Eph 2: 1ff). It is through the work of the Holy Spirit that we have been made 'alive' to God (John 3:5–8; Tit 3:5f) and made members of God's family, with the right to call God 'Abba' (Rom 8:14–16; Gal 4:6). Moreover, communication with God can take place only through the mediation of the Spirit (cf Rom 8:26; 1 Cor 2: 10ff; Phil 3:3) and that is why it is essential that all worship is inspired and prompted by him (cf John 4:24; 1 Cor 12:7; 14:26; Eph 5:18f; 6:18). It is the Spirit who takes the things of God and makes them real to us (cf John 16:1–15) so that we are impelled to respond in worship.

THE FORM OF WORSHIP

In this second part, we narrow down our consideration of 'worship' to the *corporate* aspect of the worship of the people of God, to the things they do when they consciously meet together in the presence of God.

Biblical practice

The following brief summary makes no attempt to be comprehensive. As far as Jewish practices are concerned, it deals largely with worship in the sanctuary (taking together the whole period from Moses to 70 AD) and in the synagogue. It hardly notices the aspects of individual worship at other times and places, nor does it deal with practices in the time of the Judges (eg Judg 17:5) and the place of worship on the battlefield (cf Exod 15; 1 Sam 7:5ff; 13:8ff; 2 Chron 20; Pss 20; 44; 74).

Patriarchal worship

Pre-Mosaic worship is depicted as largely individual (cf Gen 4: 3ff; 8:20) or representative, with the clan father offering sacrifices and prayers on behalf of his family (cf Job 1:5; Gen 22:5; 35:2–7). Altars, trees and pillars figure in this early worship (cf Gen 12:8; 21:33; 28:18): it seems that some use was made of contemporary modes of worship.

Tabernacle and temple worship

DESIGN AND DETAILS
The tabernacle was divinely prescribed (Exod. 25:8f). Its structure and furniture; its personnel and their garments; the cultic actions they were to perform; and the festivals to be celebrated: all were laid down by God (cf Exod 25–30; Lev 1–7; 16; 23; Num 8;9; 28;29; etc). There were no regulations, however, regarding words and music to be used (but cf Deut 26).

By contrast, Solomon's temple was a divine concession (cf 2 Sam 7:5ff; 1 Kings 5:3–5; 6:11; 8:15–21). He was allowed to follow David's plans, basing the overall design on that of the tabernacle but incorporating considerable Canaanite and Phoenician influences. Nevertheless, God was prepared to accept it as his house (1 Kings 8: 10f; 9:3). The organisation of singers, players and music seems to have been the result of human rather than divine direction (cf 1 Chron 15:1–24; 16:4–6; 23; 24:19).

CHARACTERISTICS

Tabernacle and temple worship was a mixture of individual, family, corporate and representative actions, with the cultic personnel assisting and leading. It centred around the bringing of animal sacrifices and other offerings, with the priests being responsible for making 'atonement' with the blood (Lev 4:30f; 17:11) and disposing of the bodies (cf Lev 1–7). The offerings expressed penitence, adoration, thanksgiving, vows, reparation, etc.

There are relatively few descriptions of a temple 'service' (cf 1 Kings 8; 2 Chron 29:2–36; Ezra 3:10f). There is also an interesting example in the Apocrypha in Ecclesiasticus 50. None gives all the details we would like to know. The psalms, however, provide a source from which we may infer further information. What is clear is that temple worship was varied, colourful, lively, exuberant, exhilarating and noisy.[1] (What with the stench of burning bodies and the cacophony of sounds, it is unlikely that *we* would have found it conducive to worship!)

OTHER CONSTITUENTS

In addition to the bringing of offerings, temple worship seems to have included: prayers – individual, corporate and representative, liturgical and spontaneous – (cf Deut 26:5f; 1 Sam 1:10f; 1 Kings 8:23ff); singing (choir only?) with instrumental accompaniment and 'breaks' (cf Ezra 3:10ff; Psa 150 etc and 'selahs'); shouting (Ezra 3:11); clapping (?cf Psa 47:1); dancing (cf Exod 15:20; 2 Sam 6:14; 1 Chron 15:29; Pss 149:3; 150:4; Jer 31:13); drama (cf Ps 48:9); processions (cf Neh 12:31ff; Pss 48: 12f; 55:14; 118:27); historical and credal recitations (cf Deut 6:4ff; 26:5ff; Pss 105; 106); priestly instruction and prophetic exhortation (cf Psa 78; Jer 7); covenant renewal (cf Josh 24; Neh 10; Psa 50); fasts (cf Joel 1:14); vigils (cf Psa 134:1; Joel 1:13); silence (Pss 4:4; 46:10; 76:8); and priestly blessing (cf Num 6:22ff; 1 Kings 8:55).

POSTURES

Presumably the full range of possible postures and gestures were used in public as well as private worship: standing (2 Chron 20:9);

---

1. H H Rowley describes it as 'organized noise making' in *Worship in Ancient Israel*, SPCK, 1967, 206.

sitting (2 Sam 7:18); kneeling (Psa 95:6); prostrating (Job 1:20); raising hands (Psa 134:2); and spreading out the hands (Ezra 9:5).

Synagogue worship

Whatever the origins of the synagogue, it became an alternative to the temple for those unable to travel to Jerusalem. It could never replace the temple (because only there could animal sacrifices be offered), but it developed into a centre for the reading and study of the Torah (Law) in a setting of praise and prayer (which was regarded as the equivalent of the temple sacrifices), and thus became the normal place of worship for the majority of Jews (even before the destruction of the second temple).

Its services were led by various lay officials with opportunity for any male to take part (although it appears that, gradually, prayers became less spontaneous and more liturgical). A typical service would include prayers; the *Shema* (Deut 6:4ff); a reading from the Torah (Pentateuch); a reading from the Prophets; translations and a sermon; singing of psalms; benedictions and a blessing.

Early church worship

The closest we get in the New Testament to a description of a Christian 'service' (or rather 'meeting', cf 1 Cor 11: 17ff) is Acts 20:7–11. This and other, passing, references (such as in 1 Cor 11–16) are hardly sufficient to enable us properly to reconstruct or visualise early Christian worship. Outside the New Testament we have valuable evidence in the *Didache* (chs 6–16, probably late first century or early second), the *Apology* of Justin (I.65–67, c 150 AD) and Pliny's *Letter* to Trajan (X.96, c 112 AD).

It would seem that early Christian worship was largely influenced by the synagogue, with only marginal Gentile influence. It is also very likely that the example of Jesus and, especially, the form and content of the Last Supper and the upper room ministry (Luke 22:7–38; John 13:2–18:1) exerted a considerable influence. In addition, we cannot assume uniformity and thus we must make allowance for the possibility of a variety of forms and practices in the early church.

THE JERUSALEM CHURCH

It would seem that the early Christians continued to attend the temple and the synagogue, not simply as convenient meeting-places but in order to join in Jewish worship (cf Luke 24:53; Acts 1:15; 2:46;

3:1; 5:42; 21:24ff). Specifically Christian worship took place in homes (Acts 1:13; 2:46; 4:23; 12:12). Acts 2:42 may well describe the usual constituents of such worship: teaching; 'fellowship' (lit 'sharing' – probably, either a collection for the poor or – more likely – a common meal in which the better off shared with the less well off); 'breaking of bread' (probably the remembrance of the Lord at the beginning and ending of the meal); prayer (lit 'the prayers', probably both spontaneous and fixed, and including the singing of psalms; cf Acts 4:24–30).

Baptisms presumably took place in public (cf Acts 2:41), but we have no detailed description of a 'baptismal service' (cf Acts 8:36ff). Of the conduct of marriages and funerals (they must have had them!) we have no evidence whatsoever: we assume that current Jewish practices were simply taken over and 'Christianized'. Similarly, there is little solid evidence as to whether the early Christians continued to keep the sabbath and the Jewish festivals, or whether they began to develop a Christian calendar, with emphasis on the first day of the week.

THE PAULINE CHURCHES

The core of Paul's converts were Jews and proselytes. It is unlikely that they were often able to continue attending the synagogue, but it is quite likely that their meetings for worship in each other's homes (cf 1 Cor 16:19; Col 4:15) were modelled to a large extent on synagogue practice.

The Sunday (Saturday?) evening meeting in Troas described in Acts 20:7–12 included teaching (extensive!) and the Lord's Supper (probably as part of a communal meal). 1 Corinthians gives further insight into Christian meetings for worship in which the Lord's Supper formed part of a communal meal (cf 1 Cor 11:17–22) and in which scope was given for the exercise of various spiritual gifts (1 Cor 14:26), the use of which, however, could easily lead to chaotic conditions that called for some degree of control (by the leaders? cf 1 Cor 14:2–29). The extent of women's participation is still debated (cf 1 Cor 11:5ff; 14:34ff; 1 Tim 2:9ff). Meetings apparently took place on Sunday (as well as at other times?) and included (if appropriate) a collection (1 Cor 16: 1ff).

References in the Pauline letters point to the use of a variety of songs, some traditional, some newly composed, and some spontaneous (cf Eph 5:19; Col 3:16); and, at times, Paul may actually be quoting from early Christian hymns (eg, Phil 2:5ff; Col 1:15ff; 1 Tim 3:16). We can be quite confident, also, that prayers were similarly both fixed and extempore (cf Eph 6: 18f; Col 4:2ff; 1 Tim 2: 1ff, 8), and that we catch a glimpse of early Christian praying in the recorded prayers of Paul (eg, Eph 3: 14ff). Paul's use of the Aramaic '*Abba*' and '*Marana tha*' (Rom 8:15; Gal 4:6; 1 Cor 16:22) may well echo ejaculatory words and phrases (including also 'Amen' and 'Hallelujah'?) used in worship.

THE JOHANNINE CHURCHES:

The heavenly songs in the book of Revelation may reflect the worship of the churches in Asia. It is also possible that John's Gospel throws light on the content and emphases of the worship in the circles from which it emanated.

Biblical principles

Having looked at some of the ways in which God's people have worshipped him in the past, we come now to consider how *we* should worship him. How can we be sure that our worship pleases God? Has he told us how he likes to be worshipped? Can we discover in the Bible a pattern for our worship?

Pattern or principles?

OLD TESTAMENT

It is generally agreed that the pattern of worship ordained for, or adopted by, Israel is not binding on Christians. It is not simply that Jesus has fulfilled or superseded the ceremonial laws and, especially, the institution of animal sacrifice (cf Matt 5:17; Mark 7:18–19; Heb 7:18–19; 10:1–10), but that the church is not Israel. What was written in the Old Testament scriptures was written for our *learning* (Rom 15:4; 2 Tim 3:16), not necessarily for our *imitation*. What we learn from the Old Testament descriptions of worship, as well as from the exhortations to, and expressions of, worship (eg, in the psalms), are the basic spiritual principles that should govern our practice of worship.

NEW TESTAMENT:

In what way is the New Testament different from the Old? Is it written for our imitation as well as for our learning? If we could discover exactly how the early church worshipped, would that constitute a blueprint that we would be obliged to follow? Or should we distinguish between what is *described* in the New Testament (eg, in Acts) and what *is commanded* (eg, in the epistles)? For example, fasting is described in Acts (13:3) but not actually commanded in the epistles; whereas singing is commanded (Eph 5:19) but nothing is said about musical accompaniment.

The main forms or expressions of worship which are actually commanded (as opposed to being described), either by Jesus himself or by the apostles, are: baptism (Matt 28:19); the Lord's Supper (Luke 22: 19f; 1 Cor 11:2–26); singing (Eph 5:19; Col 3:16); praying (1 Thess 5:17); giving thanks (Col 3:17); using spiritual gifts (1 Cor 14:26); teaching (1 Tim 4:13); reading the scriptures (1 Tim 4:13); taking a collection (1 Cor 16:2); giving a holy kiss (1 Thess 5:26); and washing each other's feet (John 13:14).

In no case are there detailed instructions on how these actions or activities are to be performed, except that some guidance is given on the exercise of certain spiritual gifts (1 Cor 14) and on what is unacceptable practice in relation to the Lord's Supper (1 Cor 10;11). The main directions regarding the conduct of worship relate almost exclusively to the participation and clothing of women (1 Cor 11 :5ff; 14:34f; 1 Tim 2:9ff). James 2, however, does deal with where people should sit in a church service!

The consequence is that, if we look for a detailed pattern for Christian worship in the New Testament, we shall be disappointed. There is just *not* sufficient detail. If we adopt the approach that 'nothing is permitted unless it is commanded', we shall deprive ourselves of much that is helpful and conducive to real worship. If we try to copy all the procedures of the early church, we shall find that some of them do not fit our culture or circumstances. (It is ironic that some who have claimed to be basing their worship on the New Testament pattern have spiritualized 'feet-washing'; reinterpreted the 'holy kiss' as a handshake; and refused to acknowledge the validity of some of the gifts mentioned in 1 Corinthians 14:26, while using that verse as the justification for 'open' worship!) Worst of all, this approach leads to Pharisaism, an emphasis on externals, pride in being 'correct' and judgment of others who differ.

Although there are clearly a number of constituents which are essential to Christian worship (or at least, highly desirable), it would seem more realistic and appropriate to regard both the detailed instructions about and the more general descriptions of worship contained in the New Testament as contemporary applications of spiritual principles rather than as rules binding on the church for all time.

Acceptable forms of worship

Are we, therefore, free to express our worship in any form we choose or that appeals to us? Are there any limits, or is anything potentially permissible? There are three principles that seem to be fundamental.

1. WORSHIP SHOULD BE 'IN SPIRIT AND IN TRUTH' (JOHN 4:24)

Since worship is primarily for God, it should please him and bring him glory. The problem is: how do we know what pleases God? The scriptural answer is that God is interested primarily in *heart* worship, in the *inward* thoughts and feelings of a person, and is concerned about the outward forms only in so far as they express or enable true inward worship (cf Psa 51:17; Isa 29:13; John 4:23f; Eph 5:19). Thus, for example, God enjoys our singing only if it really expresses the feelings of our hearts towards him.

Worship should be 'in truth' not only in the sense that it is 'sincere' but also that it is in accordance with the truth about God, as revealed in the Bible. Acceptable worship is a response to and a mirroring of the nature and character of God (cf Heb 12:18f).

Above all, God has made it clear that no worship (however deeply felt) is acceptable unless it is the expression of a life lived in 'truth', that is, in obedience to him (cf Pss 15; 24; 50; Isa 1: 1–17; Jer 7:22f; Hos 6:6; Amos 5:2lff; Mic 6:6ff; Matt 5:23f; 1 John 1:6; 2:4; 4:20; 5:3). As Augustine is supposed to have said, 'Make sure your life sings the same tune as your mouth'.

2. WORSHIP (NORMALLY) INVOLVES SOME PHYSICAL EXPRESSION

Since we are physical beings and normally express our thoughts and feelings by means of our bodies, worship (particularly corporate worship) will usually involve some physical activities. (That does not mean that someone who is totally paralysed cannot worship God!) In addition, it should be recognised that physical gestures may not only *express* feelings but also *generate* them (cf a kiss; 'making love').

How much or what kind of physical expression is felt necessary and appropriate will no doubt depend partly on personality, temperament, age, experience, cultural background, education and so on. (It cannot be accidental that the forms of worship that God imposed on Israel were so similar in many respects to those of its neighbours, though there were also significant differences.)

Because we find it hard to concentrate on one thing for long, and because we soon get into a routine, and worship can so easily become a mere formality, we need variety in the content and forms of our worship (cf OT worship in the temple).

3. CORPORATE WORSHIP SHOULD BE AN EXPRESSION OF UNITY
(ROM 15:6; 1 COR 10:17)

If God is looking for the *united* worship of his people, anything that disrupts or destroys that unity renders the worship unacceptable (cf 1 Cor 11:17–22). It is, therefore, essential not only that there should be right relationships between Christians (cf Psa 133; Matt 5:25; Eph 4:2–6; Phil 2: 1–4) but also that each person should be able to participate as fully as possible in the worship and use his/her gifts for the benefit of the others (Rom 12:3–8; 1 Cor 12:7–11).

Testing our worship

We close with a check-list of the kind of questions that we should ask about any proposed form of worship. The questions are based on the principles which scripture provides for testing the acceptability of our worship.

- Is it compatible with the revealed nature and will of God? (Cf Deut 4:15ff; 18:9ff; 1 Kings 12:26–33)

- Does it express and encourage a reverential attitude to God? (Cf Psa 22:23; Heb 12:28)

- Does it direct attention to God rather than to others or oneself? (Cf Matt 6:1–6; Col 2:18f)

- Does it foster an awareness of God's presence? (Cf 1 Cor 14:24f)

- Does it centre on the person and work of Christ? (Cf John 5:23; Phil 2:10f; Col 1:15ff)

- Does it increase people's appreciation of God – Father, Son and Holy Spirit? (Cf Eph 1:17ff; 3:14ff)

- Is it inspired and prompted by the Holy Spirit? (Cf John 4:23f; Eph 5:18ff)

- Does it allow freedom for the Holy Spirit to direct, modify or inhibit? (Cf John 16:13f; Gal 5:16,25)

- Does it enable God to communicate with his people? (Cf 1 Cor 14:19; Col 3:16; 1 Thess 5:19)

- Does it express what people actually think and feel about God? (Cf Isa 29:13)

- Does it facilitate united, corporate worship? (Cf Rom 15:5f)

- Does it leave room for individual response and decision? (Cf Rom 14:5,23; 1 Cor 14:29; Col 2:16; 1 Thess 5:21)

- Does it lead to intelligent (as well as felt) worship? (Cf John 4:24; 1 Cor 14:6–19)

- Does it strengthen people for service? (Cf 1 Cor 14:12; Eph 4:12)

- Does it involve cost or sacrifice? (Cf 2 Sam 24:24; Mark 14:3ff)

- Does it make use of *all* the gifts that God has given to this particular congregation? (Cf 1 Cor 14:26)

- Can it be done in a decent and orderly way, in submission to one another and to the leaders? (Cf 1 Cor 14:33,40; Eph 5:21; Heb 13:17)

- Is it morally acceptable? (Cf Deut 23:17f; 1 Cor 11:21ff)

- Does it lead to a life of obedience? (Cf Col 2:23; Jas 1:26f)

- Does it glorify God in the eyes of unbelievers? (Cf Matt 5:16; 1 Cor 14:24f; 1 Pet 2:9)

Worship is the greatest privilege that is granted to the people of God. We must do our utmost to ensure that it is as pleasing to God as we can make it.

We are here to praise You,
Lift our hearts and sing.
We are here to give You
The best that we can bring.

And it is our love
Rising from our hearts,
Everything within us cries:
'Abba Father.'

Help us now to give You
Pleasure and delight.
Heart and mind and will that say:
'I love You Lord,'[1]

---

1. Graham Kendrick, Thank You Music, 1985.

2

The practice of worship: biblical and historical

Neil Summerton

As elder of a local church, Neil Summerton writes on the basis of long experience of the practice and conduct of worship. He is the author of A Noble Task: Eldership and Ministry in the Local Church. *For many years he was an under-secretary in the Department of the Environment in the United Kingdom. Recently, he moved to be director of the Oxford Centre for the Environment, Ethics and Society at Mansfield College Oxford.*

INTRODUCTION

Not the least of the distinctive features of the New Testament church was the character of its worship. From what little we are told, it appears that the worship of the early church was decisively different from that of both first-century Judaism and the various cults to be found in the Gentile culture of the day. Of course, this distinctiveness took a little time to establish itself. The Christians in Jerusalem continued for some time in temple worship as well as prayer and worship among themselves as Christians (Acts 2:46; 3:1; 21:26). And the synagogue can be seen to have had some influence upon the worship of the early church, just as it did upon its organization.

But the worship of both the Hebrew temple and the pagan temple was characterized by prescribed forms and activities, and by pre-determined content, performed by specially selected individuals. Furthermore, it took place in a special building or place set aside (consecrated) for the purpose. By contrast, the early church did without special places for worship; permitted or encouraged partici-pation in worship widely by those attending; and clearly left much latitude to participants to decide the form and content of the worship event. We should not, however, assume that all worship was spontaneous in the early church – evidence of pre-formulated worship material can be discerned in the pages of the New Testament.[1]

New Testament worship was consistent with the radical dissolution of the distinction between the sacred and secular which was characteristic of the Pentecostal age (and which, it can be argued, is a characteristic at all times of revival and other significant movements of the Holy Spirit). The normal place of worship was not special but in people's houses and on occasion, elsewhere, for example, on the river bank (Acts 12:12–17; 16:13; 18:7; 20:7; Rom. 16:5; 1 Cor. 11:17–32). There was great freedom of form and content, as can be seen, particularly, from the account of the worship at Troas (Acts 20: 7–12) and at Corinth where, clearly, Paul is describing the normal worship of the Corinthian church (1 Cor 14). Prophetic utterance was also a regular, not to say normal, occurrence in the gatherings of the New Testament church.

If all the references are taken together we can see that, in the New Testament, there is no sharp distinction between meetings of the local church (congregation) as such, meetings of part of it, and meetings which in traditional 'Brethren' parlance would have been considered 'private' or unofficial.[2] Rather, there is a flexible continuum from small and, no doubt, impromptu gatherings in the homes of individuals to larger gatherings, possibly in the commodious home of a well-to-do member of the congregation, possibly in a particular part of the temple precinct in Jerusalem, possibly in the fields. All were meetings of 'the church', the form and character of the events to some extent depending, no doubt, on the circumstances and scale of the particular gathering. All, it might be added, must in principle have been equally subject to the leadership and authority of the church, in particular as to doctrine and the Pauline injunction, for example, that 'all things should be done decently and in order' (1 Cor 14:40).[3]

1. See Ralph Martin, *Worship in the Early Church*, 1974, 28–65.
2. In this way of thinking, a church meeting was only such if it was intended for all the members of a particular fellowship in its normal place of meeting. A meeting of some members in a private home was not regarded as a meeting of the church, nor under its jurisdiction. This was, perhaps, one reason for the widespread resistance, twenty years ago, to home groups.
3. Thus, there is no reason in our day why midweek house groups for worship, Bible study and fellowship should be construed as inevitably divisive or outside the authority of the congregation. That anxiety derives, I suspect, from a distinction between corporate and private activity which has more to do with Victorian notions of the Englishman's home as his castle than it does with the New Testament – though, of course, where such notions are strongly held, there might be good reason for caution about the development of groups which might be outside effective regulation by the congregation.

This flexible pattern of worship did not last long in the church. Just as sacerdotalism began to be discernible in certain parts of the church before the end of the first century, so formal liturgies also began to emerge quickly. These were possibly parallel and self-reinforcing phenomena, since a distinct clergy is helped in establishing its special position by having a formal liturgy which it alone is qualified to perform.

This formalization can be seen in other aspects of church life, such as the discontinuance of immediate baptism in favour of the rigorous preparation of candidates for baptism annually on Easter Sunday. There were good practical reasons for some of this, just as the phenomenal growth of the early church in some places made it sensible to meet, not in homes but in specially reserved and, soon, specially designed buildings. Frequently, those special buildings were modelled on the lay-out of the synagogue and in time, it has to be said, they were influenced, too, by the lay-out of the pagan temples with which so many converts were familiar. This trend was reinforced, it may be surmised, by the theological move towards sacerdotalism.

The influence of familiar structures and practices on any group of Christians is inevitable. We ourselves have been affected by it. The 'Brethren' oversight of the nineteenth century can be seen, from one point of view, not so much as an effort to return to the principles of the New Testament as an application of one of the characteristic institutions of Victorian England – the committee. (So was the parochial church council invented for the Anglicans by William Temple and others in 1921!) Strange as it may seem to us, the 'Brethren' gospel meeting of the nineteenth century consciously made use of popular cultural forms. In our own day, I am struck by the similarities between the physical and phonetic manifestations to be seen and heard on the video tapes of rock concerts which my children play, and those to be found at Christian celebrations, such as those at the annual Spring Harvest event (though the latter is now sobering down somewhat!). In itself, this cultural contextualisation is no bad thing – rather the reverse. If worship is to be meaningful to the individual and the group, it must be expressed in an intellectual and emotional idiom with which they can identify.

But on the question of worship, as on other matters, the church and its leadership had better be on its guard. The genius of the New Testament is that it does not seek to legitimize and sacralize any particular form or way of doing things in worship. Rather, in sharp contrast to both the Hebrew and Gentile worship of the first century, it presents the radically-new goal of a worship which, in the Holy Spirit, is vibrant, dynamic, alive, and unrestricted by form, place and person.

The history of the church suggests that, in periods of revival and restoration, efforts are usually made to recover the New Testament character of worship. As the fires of spiritual intensity burn down, however, formalization of worship re-establishes itself. The church tends to revert to the forms of religious institutionalization which are common to fallen man. So it re-establishes a caste of 'holy' men to lead or perform worship, 'sacred' places for worship, and 'sacred' formularies for worship. In short, it tends to re-establish the dichotomy between the sacred and the secular which the Christian spirit and mind of the New Testament simply refused to recognise.[1]

It needs to be emphasized that this process can be as true of unstructured, non-formal and participatory worship, as it is of worship which relies on written formularies. The challenge for all local churches, of whatever type, is how to keep their collective worship and prayer vibrant, dynamic, alive, and unrestricted by form, place and person. That can only be done, in my judgment, if it is in touch with the idioms and characteristic modes of expression of the worshippers, and is at the same time thoroughly in touch with the living triune God as revealed in the scriptures. To put the point another way, provided that there is no heresy, there is every reason why each particular group of Christians should be free to worship in their own distinctive way, so long as they are authentically in touch with the Lord as he is revealed in scripture, and they avoid the formalization and institutionalisation (in the sense of ossification) of worship.

It is absolutely crucial that the worship experience of each local church, of whatever kind, should, by meeting these twin criteria, be kept spiritually alive. That is essential for the spiritual growth of the members and for the growth of the fellowship through the addition of those who are already Christians. The reality is that, in our mobile societies, many come 'worshipping with a view' to membership – they will stay only if they think that the fellowship offers what they

---

1. On this process, see John Tiller with Mark Birchall, *The Gospel Community and its Leadership*, 1987, 1–51.

need, including worship that is 'real'. Regrettable as it may perhaps be, in our consumerist age, if Christians feel that God is not present in the worship of a local church, they will not stay long but will search elsewhere for a fellowship where they consider that he is present.

Such worship is essential, too, if non-Christians, and others on the fringe, are to be added to the fellowship – just as much as, in the first century, it was essential that unbelievers, seeing the church at worship, should 'fall down and worship God, exclaiming, "God is really among you!"' (1 Cor 14:25).[1] It is essential that worship should be 'seeker-friendly' for both believers and non-believers (though I say more below about how 'seeker-friendly' should be defined in this context).

Before turning (in the next chapter) to discuss how local churches which are the particular subject of Partnership literature can best be helped towards these objectives, we need to analyse where collective worship now stands in the particular fellowship of which we are members.

WORSHIP IN PARTNERSHIP-TYPE CHURCHES

Such analysis can only be done by the reader in relation to his or her own fellowship. The writer cannot do more than sketch out a number of general possibilities, in the hope that they may assist the reader in locating his or her own fellowship on the 'worship map', as it might be termed.

When the first edition of this book appeared ten years ago, the character of worship in churches of 'Brethren' background was such that I found it necessary only to fill out that part of the map of then-current practice which related to the traditional formularies of 'Brethren' worship. That sheet is still required for our journey – there are still many churches of 'Brethren' background where the assumptions about and practice of worship owe much to the theory and practice of such churches, as they developed over the period 1830–1980. So I include my earlier analysis with comparatively ltttle modification.

---

1. Paul was clear, of course, that prophecy was the key feature of worship that would produce this effect (see the context of the verses cited).

But the position is changing rapidly in local churches of this background, and we need, therefore, to refer also to two other adaptations of worship that have appeared over the last twenty years in many of these churches. For convenience, I term them, 'Charismatic' style worship', and 'entertainment-worship' including the so-called 'family service' and the 'seeker-friendly' service.

Traditional 'Brethren' worship

Two different, co-habiting traditions of worship can, in my judgment, be discerned in 'Brethren' congregations or those of 'Brethren' background. They can today still be found in many such congregations in different parts of at least the Anglo-Saxon world. These two traditions have different spiritual roots.

Roots

First, there is a tradition of spontaneous or 'open' worship which 'Brethren' adherents would regard as both the characteristic form of 'Brethren' worship and the normative form of Christian worship. Traditionally, it has been practised at the meeting known as the Lord's Supper or the Breaking of Bread, and in the weekly prayer meeting. This method derives from the efforts of the founders of the movement in the 1830s and 1840s to return to what they regarded as the authentic character of worship as depicted in the pages of the New Testament.

For particular reasons relating to the specific origins of the movement, manifestations such as prophecy and tongue-speaking were rejected as appropriate practice in this worship. But its character was essentially charismatic, in that it looked directly to the Holy Spirit to lead audible participation in worship and, accordingly, allowed for a wide measure of contribution from the congregation (though in the early days a presidency with, in essence, a 'police power' to control unhelpful contribution was practised in some places[1]).

A similar openness was also practised with respect to the ministry of the word, in the midweek ministry meeting, the conversational Bible study, and the Saturday inter-congregational conferences which were regularly held and which were one of the principal

---

1. F Roy Coad, *A History of the Brethren Movement*, second edition, 1976, 125–126, 128; H H Rowdon, *The Origins of the Brethren 1825–1850*, 1967, 227–228.

mechanisms by which the movement acquired coherence as a denomination. Knowledge of the practice is now being lost in the mists of time, but it was the case that, even at these inter-congregational conferences, often no speaker was booked in advance – though one suspects that sometimes there was a certain amount of stage-management through the clandestine invitation of a distinguished speaker to whom others were expected to yield place![1]

The second mode of worship derived from the alternative and quantitatively far more important source of the 'Brethren' movement – the revivals of the latter part of the nineteenth century associated in particular with the names of Moody and Sankey and perhaps, later, with Torrey and Alexander. Subsequently, these influences were reinforced by the Keswick experience and by participation in ventures such as the CSSM. These associations were as important as 'Brethren' theology in determining the characteristic spirituality of the movement, and they provided both the hymnology of the movement (at events other than the Breaking of Bread meeting) and a highly structured form of worship with strong leadership from the platform. This structure with, for example, the singing of choruses 'while people are coming in' was, I suspect, very much modelled on the pattern of the revivalist meeting to which Moody and Sankey were heirs.

Undoubtedly, the pattern of 'open' worship would have been considered the superior form, and it is doubtful whether many would have thought of what went on at the gospel meeting as being worship – though it clearly was, and it can be argued that the undoubted success in its day of that meeting as a vehicle of evangelism owed much to the reality of worship expressed by the Christians present. That reality owed not a little to the fact that the worship was cast in a cultural form that struck a chord with both them and the unbelievers present.

Recent expression

Among the Protestant sects, the 'Open Brethren' have been remarkably successful in maintaining their vigour and spiritual vitality over a period of some five or six generations (in other groups, the rate of spiritual decline and departure from evangelical truth has often

1. As late as 1959, G H Lang thought it necessary to defend the principle of the open platform at conferences (G H Lang, *The Churches of God: their constitution, discipline and ministry*, 1959, 81–91).

tended to be more rapid). Nevertheless, it is scarcely surprising that, over such a long period, many features of its denominational life should have ossified into debilitating traditions. In no aspect has this been more true than in its worship. Despite the rejection of written formularies, of special sacred buildings, and of a special sacred caste, the tendency has been to institutionalize to such a degree that sacred and secular compartments in the lives of the worshippers have been re-established.

Nowhere has this rigidity been seen more clearly than in the Breaking of Bread meeting, as practised in at least the last two generations. Still, in many places, that event is widely regarded (with some biblical justification of course) as being central in the life of the congregation. In consequence, nothing should, it is often argued, dethrone it from its place in the weekly calendar – certainly not the task of evangelism, for example. It becomes the central cultic act. Attendance at it becomes as mandatory as that of the Catholic at weekly Mass. It may even be regarded as virtually the exclusive measure of an individual's spiritual state. Some take this view to the point that, though they have no effective fellowship with the congregation concerned and, indeed, may be at loggerheads with it doctrinally and personally, they would never dream of missing the Breaking of Bread meeting.

In form, the meeting (and indeed the prayer meeting) has generally come to be dominated by a rigid, though unwritten, liturgy. Though there are variations between congregations, in any one of them the order of the event is utterly predictable. It will almost certainly begin with a hymn. That hymn will determine the theme and content of the remaining period of worship. There will be a prayer of institution before the bread is taken, and a similar prayer before the wine is taken. The offering will be taken up immediately following; and, if there is arranged or 'spontaneous' ministry, it will then follow. The prayer of institution for the bread will begin at an accustomed time, give or take a minute or two. The whole event will conclude at a particular time (justified, of course, on the grounds of convenience and practicality). If anyone moves outside this time-table the body language of emotional and intellectual discomfort will be all too obvious in the congregation – for example, if a hymn or song is proposed after the elements have been passed round, or possibly while they are being passed round!

The form and content of worship are also restricted. The

limitation on content can be traced to the view that the meeting is in memory of the Lord's *death*, so that any worship material which does not meet this single criterion is considered to be inappropriate. In consequence, a homiletic contribution or an individual's spiritual experience of the Lord is ruled out. So is a word of personal testimony from a young person, as to what the Lord has done for them recently. So, too, is thanksgiving for any matter which is not directly related to the work of Christ on the cross. The same principle can be seen at work in relation to the use of scripture and song in open worship at the Lord's table. The material *must* focus narrowly on the Lord's death. Readings, hymns, ministry which turn the congregation's mind towards the Father, or towards the glory of God, or towards his kingdom which is at once now and not yet, is unacceptable. If anyone dares to introduce this type of material, others will quickly bring the meeting back to content which is considered appropriate to the occasion, and the perpetrator may get a rap across the knuckles afterwards!

If acceptable content is narrow, so is form. Expositional preaching of the word in the course of worship is often considered unsuitable, and one suspects that, in some places, homiletic preaching or, indeed, any human enlargement upon the meaning of scripture is frowned upon. In many places, the form has settled down into a sandwich of hymn, prayer and scripture reading, punctuated by long (often empty) silences, and it would be thought odd even to propose that one hymn should be followed immediately by another. Often, oral participation is limited for want of (male) numbers to a handful of individuals who are themselves only too conscious that there are limitations on the spiritual variety which they are capable of bringing to the worship event.

The problems of limitation of form are not, in my view, limited to highly traditional approaches to worship. Efforts, 25 and 30 years ago, to modernize worship have brought their own problems. Though highly necessary at the time, the instruments then introduced to accompany worship at the Lord's table (the piano and the organ – in most places they had, of course, been used at evangelistic meetings since the last century) have proved to be highly inflexible. So have the collections of hymns then favoured, largely on grounds of their theological and intellectual depth. Valuable though these developments were in their time, they have resulted in an inflexibility in worship, and often severe interruptions in the spiritual 'flow' of worship. Congregations are tied intellectually, manually and visually to their hymnbooks and can apparently do nothing in worship without waiting for the accompanist to find the tune and strike it up on the instrument.

The same kind of problems can afflict meetings for prayer. Here, too, the range of content is narrow. The event is often seen as being narrowly intended for *intercessory* prayer, and material which concentrates on worship is considered misplaced from the worship services of the congregation. Where this is combined with an unwillingness to engage in deep supplication for the specific needs of individual members of the fellowship and for the fellowship as a whole, the result is arid meetings in which a dull and unspecific shopping list of requirements is presented to the Lord. Again there are extensive empty silences punctuated by a few lengthy contributions by the 'professional' pray-ers of the congregation. There is little worship and thanksgiving, and little sense of the corporate nature of prayer in which the baton of prayer is eagerly and urgently taken up from one to another.

Things are frequently little or no better at gospel or teaching meetings which are prepared and led, usually by the person appointed to preach at the occasion. Preparatory hymn and song singing has rightly been abandoned as no longer serving a useful purpose. This is usually because it no longer catches the idiom in which people wish to worship. It is interesting that, in some circles where there is manifestly a spirit of worship, preparatory singing of spiritual songs is widely to be found. Once the 'service proper' has begun (significant terminology in itself), an unwritten nonconformist liturgy is generally followed. It comprises hymns interspersed with prayers and Bible readings, leading in due course to the preaching of the word – the familiar 'hymn-prayer sandwich'. Apart from the notices, individual contribution in prayer and reading is confined to the 'chairman'/speaker, and congregational expression is confined to collective hymn singing. Frequently it is all too obvious that what precedes the address is viewed as no more than preparatory to it. These preliminaries are not thought of as capable of standing on their own as a sufficient end in themselves – if they were the only purpose of coming together, we would not bother.

Finally, singing is confined to collections of hymns such as *Hymns of Faith, Christian Worship, Christian Praise* or even, still, *The Golden*

Hymnal, Sacred Songs and Solos, or *Redemption Hymns*. Accompaniment is by means of a single 'heavy' instrument. All these were, of course, dynamic innovations in their day and, so far as hymns are concerned, there is no doubt that the church can make much good use of the forms of expression in which earlier generations of Christians chose to cast their spiritual experience. But if this material becomes the sole means of our spiritual expression, then we shall be being truly liturgical, ie, casting our worship in traditional formularies, albeit in the undoubtedly worthy ones of the first to fourth evangelical revivals. I would assert that there is something seriously wrong if a group of Christians do not cast at least some of their corporate expressions of fellowship in forms which are original to themselves. Otherwise, they are likely to be living on past spiritual capital, not their present experience of the Lord.

In summarising the character of the corporate spiritual exercises which have been commonly found in Brethren congregations in Britain, I would point to three key features.

First, they have an essentially cerebral nature. It is as though the previous generation took too seriously to heart John Henry Newman's criticism of the Evangelicalism in which both Brethrenism and Tractarianism were rooted, viz, that it was guilty of shallow emotionalism.[1] It is doubtful, in fact, if the 'Brethren' of the late nineteenth and early twentieth century could have been charged with being over-cerebral but, by way of reaction in the last two generations, there seems to have been a fear of engaging the emotions in worship, and certainly of permitting any significant *physical* expression of worship. These have often been rejected as associated with the (allegedly unbiblical) over-exuberance of ethnic, Pentecostal and 'Charismatic' groups.

Second, even when spiritual exercises are cast in a form in which worship is intended to be spontaneous under the leadership of the Holy Spirit, there is often – even normally – a fundamental lack of spontaneity. Rather, there is a predictability about the event which is discouraging. It will be known who will take part, roughly when, and the content will be all too familiar, There is a reluctance to break out of the accustomed form. Worship has in fact become fundamentally liturgical in character.

---

1. See C S Dessain, *John Henry Newman*, 1966, in particular the material cited from *Parochial and Plain Sermons* on pages 17–21.

Third, worship in many 'Brethren' churches has a distinctive mood which is partly attributable to the content which is thought to be appropriate in worship. There is a lack of joy and vibrancy. Frequently, the dominant sentiment is of melancholia which, in my judgment, the tradition imbibed from one strand of Victorian romanticism rather than from scripture. This melancholia encourages and feeds on a sense of spiritual depression and hopelessness which are symptomatic of the parlous state into which the movement has fallen in the last two generations. This is well illustrated by the comment of a visitor from another spiritual tradition who arrived in good time for a Breaking of Bread service. After a few moments, he jokingly remarked to his hostess, 'It feels as though we are waiting for a funeral'. After ten minutes of worship, he was compelled to comment, now with deadly earnestness, 'We *are* at a funeral!'. Even if the story is apocryphal, it catches well the tenor of worship in the recent past in many churches of 'Brethren' background.

'Charismatic' worship

I have dwelt at length on the character of traditional 'Brethren' worship because many congregations of that background are still wrestling with the problems of rejuvenating these traditions and struggling to adapt them to modern needs.

But, in the last twenty years, a sea-change has occurred in the character of many Evangelical worship occasions in the United Kingdom and in many other parts of the English-speaking world. Though the origins of the style lie in the 'Charismatic'[1] movement of the last forty years, features of it have penetrated much more widely into the Evangelical community, at least in the Anglo-Saxon world, to the point that the musicology of the style is now dominant in many places. A considerable number of local churches on the 'progressive' side of the 'Brethren' movement have been influenced by these developments, even if it would be inappropriate to characterise many of those churches as 'Charismatic'.

The style has a number of key features:

---

1. I follow my usual practice of using 'Charismatic' to describe the church movement having its origins in the 1950s, and 'charismatic' to characterize the approach of giving freedom to the exercise of spiritual gifts irrespective of the particular church movement which adopts the approach.

- Song is the prominent, perhaps even the dominant feature. There is a strong implication that *only* song is worship – I have, in fact, heard it explicitly argued that prayer, the reading of scripture and other purely verbal interventions (by implication including prophecy) are a deplorable interruption of worship. In general the songs concerned (both words and tunes) are of recent composition – and it is true that many older hymns are less suitable as specifically worship vehicles because they are hymns *about* God and the Christian life, rather than being *addressed to* the Lord. (It was for a similar reason that the nineteenth-century 'Brethren' created their own hymnology and collections for worship associated with the 'Breaking of Bread'.)

- The musical accompaniment is equally modern, strong in beat, and suited to the utilisation of a wide range of musical instruments (though not, in general, strings). A competent worship band is an indispensable requirement for this style of worship (and has the merit of utilising a range of natural gifts in the particular congregation).

- Normally (though not, I would argue, indispensably – see below), this style of worship is strongly led by an individual, a 'worship-leader', usually someone of strong musical competence. It is this individual (generally male) who determines the content of the worship session, and who is the sole audible pray-er, though he may, on occasion. encourage silent or brief collective audible prayer and singing in tongues. Generally, there are no individual verbal interventions from others, either among leaders or from the body of worshippers. The 'success' of the worship session as a collective spiritual exercise is deeply dependent on the competence and spiritual sensitivity of the 'worship-leader'. (As an aid to fair assessment of this, it is worth bearing in mind, of course, that virtually throughout Christian history – though not, it should be noted, in the classical 'Brethren' teaching conference of the nineteenth century – the success of teaching and prophecy has depended on the competence and spiritual sensitivity of a single individual!).

This style of worship is, of course, consonant with an important idiom of popular culture late in the twentieth century – the pop concert (a truly global phenomenon which demonstrates the trans-cultural nature of western popular music). There we see devotees being caught up in the musical offerings of a platform band and a lead singer. The parallels with the features of worship just described are evident. To be sure, efforts have been made to offer an alternative to this style, whether liturgical or, for example, in the Taize tradition. But the key characteristic of these alternatives tends to be their elitist, intellectual character and it is hardly surprising that they do not catch on in comparison with the 'Charismatic' style. It was the genius of the 'Charismatic' movement (of the Holy Spirit, perhaps) to have opted in the last thirty years for a style of worship which was truly popular. The evidence is that many in the current generation do find it effective as a vehicle for their worship.

This new style of worship has, to my mind, contributed much to the renewal of a wide spectrum of Evangelical churches in the Anglo-Saxon world and beyond in the last twenty-five years. It has certainly encouraged a style and tone of meeting which is more accessible to the current generation than the (respective) traditional styles of Anglicanism, traditional non-conformity, and Brethrenism. It has also thereby made an important contribution to congregational evangelism. The contrast between its fundamental liveliness and people's (perhaps limited) experiences of traditional forms of Christian worship tends to guarantee that unbelievers who encounter 'Charismatic' worship often recognise that there is life there, if not God.

'Entertainment-worship'

An alternative worship form is quite widespread in Anglo-Saxon Evangelical churches. I have termed it 'entertainrnent-worship' because it seems to me that the focus of these Christian meetings is not so much upon God as upon those who attend. The aim is to bring about God-consciousness in the attender, and a sense of corporate life, by using a variety of means to communicate with them about God, Christian truth, and the life of the fellowship. In my experience, the extreme form of this approach is to be found in mainline Evangelical churches in the USA, where there can often be little opportunity for congregational participation in worship except, perhaps, for two or three congregational hymns. The remainder of the activity is performed on behalf of or, more usually, to the congregation in the form of choral pieces, interviews, reports, and, of course, preaching.

The congregation are mainly spectators, and the lay-out and use of the worship space reflects this. In this sense, this form of Protestant worship begins to have similarities with traditional Orthodox and Catholic worship, in which professionals worship on behalf of the congregation. In its extreme form, the event has the character of a TV magazine programme, or even a 'chat-show'.

As an evangelistic tool, there is much to be said for this approach. It is a form which is familar to the un-churched in their secular context (though the 'production' has to reach a high standard, if it is to compete effectively with those secular parallels, which enjoy far more production resources for a weekly half- hour programme, or a concert, than most local churches can hope to deploy). It does not make spiritual demands upon the un-churched which they feel unable to meet. It treats them in a manner with which they are perfectly familiar – that is, as consumers of a product or service about which they can make a choice (whether to come or not, and whether or not to accept what they see and hear). They need not participate in God-consciousness if they do not wish to do so.

By making Christian events 'seeker-friendly', an effort is being made, consciously or unconsciously, to evangelise. Success is, of course, likely to depend on how clear a challenge is presented at some stage, once the interest of the 'seeker' has been engaged by the nature of the event and, perhaps, the building of some kind of friendship with Christians. And it is wrong, of course, to argue that events of this style cannot in their nature lead to worship in spirit and in truth. Those who choose to accept what they hear can indeed be led to worship in their hearts – just as good teaching of the word of God has always led to such a response. [In this respect, it is wrong to characterise the Calvinist and Reformed emphasis on the word as supplanting an earlier emphasis on worship.]

'Family services' seem to me to be a variant of this form of worship event. In the case of a strict interpretation of the term[1], the consumers are a sub-group (parents and children) who, in many areas, are not necessarily strongly represented these days. The (perfectly legitimate) need to engage the attention of children tends to lay even greater stress on the entertainment element – and, of course,

---

1. There is, of course, a looser use of the term – as an event for the whole 'church family'. Such events in principle seem to me to lie somewhere between the 'seeker-friendly' event and the 'family service' strictly so-called.

on keeping it simple – which is no bad thing. [As a mentor of mine once said, 'I shall explain this for the tinies, because I find that that way the rest of us learn something!']

Nevertheless, a number of question marks must be placed against the 'entertainment' approach, particularly in a world in which, increasingly, the religious 'consumer' wishes to confine his or her involvement to one event a week, usually on Sunday morning:

- How far is it appropriate to regard the 'entertainment' approach as worship? Does it provide the opportunity for believers collectively to worship God together? Is the focus sufficiently on the Lord himself, as distinct from communicating material about him, even if it may perhaps have the effect of stimulating worship in a private, essentially unexpressed way?

- Does it give sufficient opportunity for discipling believers, both through deep worship, teaching of the word and fellowship? (It may, of course, be properly argued that reaching the lost through seeker-friendly meetings must be the priority, and that worship and discipling should be be done at other times – but if believers only appear on Sunday morning meetings what else can be done?)

- Can a short, and possibly chaotic, family service meet the needs of the majority of unbelievers present, let alone the believers?

There are, to be sure, some difficult tensions here which may not easily be resolved. Inventiveness is certainly needed – in terms of the structuring of the Sunday morning programme, and creating effective opportunities to meet some other objectives at other times.

The timing and handling of the Lord's Supper is a case in point. In my judgment, the key change that most traditional 'Brethren' churches need to make in order to see growth is to move the Breaking of Bread service away from Sunday morning, so as to be able to use that time-period differently. But some compromises are likely to be essential, too. Somehow, it is necessary to enable believers to worship, to teach believers, and to help unbelievers into the kingdom at one and the same time. It is not impossible, but it does require more time than is available in the traditional one-hour meeting, and it certainly requires that our worship events should be lively and interesting, for both believers and unbelievers.

3

The practice of worship: desirable reforms

Neil Summerton

INTRODUCTION

If the analysis of the corporate worship in many Evangelical churches today contained in the previous chapter is accurate, and if worship remains important, what is to be done to revive traditional 'Brethren' worship, and what place is to be accorded to the alternatives? Some practical suggestions follow.

Throughout, the object is to encourage a revival of deep spiritual experience when the church meets together, and not to lose the key feature of 'Brethren-style' worship as it emerged in the nineteenth century – widespread spontaneous participation in worship under the leadership of the Holy Spirit through the use of spiritual gifts. I presuppose that we ought not simply to abandon participation and the widespread use of spiritual gift in worship, in favour of either a pale imitation of 'Charismatic' worship, or 'entertainment' worship. I believe the aim should be to find meaningful, up-to-date expressions of spontaneous, Spirit-led worship, genuine congregational participation, and the free use of the relevant spiritual gifts.

TRADITIONAL SOLUTIONS

This is no new question, of course. Many who are deeply committed to traditional 'Brethren' worship are conscious that things are not quite as they ought to be. Others have been positively discontented with them for years. Wherever the barrenness of the worship service was mentioned, the answer which tended immediately to be given

in the tradition was that all could be restored if only people, especially younger people (for they are often vociferous critics of the
current state of affairs), would deepen their personal knowledge of
scripture and of the Lord in their own devotional lives and, in
particular, if they would prepare carefully beforehand rather than
spending their Saturday evenings in socialising.

There is a degree of truth in this solution. If there is a wide gap
between what is professed in corporate worship and the poverty of
spiritual experience and practice in the lives of the worshippers, it
is only to be expected that corporate worship will be hollow and
unrewarding. One thing of which we can be certain from the gospels
is that the Lord abominates spiritual and moral hypocrisy. From one
point of view, corporate worship is no more than the expression of
the reality of the day-to-day life of God's people in fellowship
together. The essential identity of worship and service in the New
Testament, as already noted, should never be forgotten.

But it is precisely because of this fact that the traditional solution
is, at best, inadequate. We are not at liberty simply to throw up our
hands and say that there is nothing to be done until individual
Christians come to a deeper and more committed spiritual life. To
do so is to propose an individualism which is common in Christianity in the West, following the Enlightenment, but which is question-
able in biblical terrns.

Throughout, scripture places great emphasis on the corporate
identity of the people of God and their corporate experience of him.
The metaphors are collective – people, nation, body, temple, assembly – and the New Testament lays great stress on fellowship and the
common life of the people together. Apart from baptism, the only
rite enjoined upon the church was a fellowship meal which empha-
sised their union *together* with the Lord (1 Cor 10:1–17). Worship was
not to be a private matter when they came together. They were to
address one *another* in psalms and hymns and spiritual songs (Eph
5:19). And one of the purposes of worship was mutual encouragement. (Heb 10:25; see also 1 Cor 14:3, which is referring to one of the
characteristic activities of the Corinthians' worship event.)

It is impossible to escape the conclusion that, typically, what the
people of God experience when they come together for worship is
something greater than they could experience privately. In fellowship, the whole is greater than the sum of the individual parts. It is
arguable that, far from worship being no stronger than the individ-

ual experiences of God represented at the gathering, the Lord reveals himself in a special way when his people meet together. Thus it is private worship which is as likely, perhaps more likely, to be enriched by the corporate worship experience than the other way round.

Second, however, the traditional solution too conveniently shifts the responsibility away from the congregational leaders and other spiritually mature members towards the young and immature. This is curious because scripture clearly places responsibility for the maturity of the church, which ought presumably to be reflected above all in its worship experience, with those who have been specially gifted for that purpose, viz, apostles, prophets, evangelists, pastors and teachers (Eph 4:11–16). Ultimately, responsibility for worship, as for every aspect of the life of a local congregation, lies with its leaders. It is they who should be seeking the Lord's guidance about the most profitable arrangements for worship. They should be teaching and encouraging others; identifying and encouraging the exercise of gift which will enrich the corporate worship of the congregation; giving a lead and modelling for all to see the kind of worship which is mutually helpful; and shepherding compassionately those who find changes in the character of worship hardest to bear.

The remainder of this essay concentrates, therefore, on the practical steps which leaders ought to take to encourage a renewal of congregational worship.

PRACTICAL STEPS

The context of worship

Despite the fact, just noted, that the worship experience of a congregation will inevitably inform and set the tone of much else in the common life of a fellowship and its individual members, it is important to remember, too, the reciprocal relationship between the various components of congregational life. Worship can, at one and the same time, be the leading edge and the summation of collective experience.

Thus in seeking a more rewarding experience, congregational leaders may have to focus on more aspects of church life than the arrangements for worship itself. The problem may be a lack of shared congregational life, with the result that the members simply come together as a collection of individuals, with little knowledge of and sympathy for each other and their concerns. There may even be a fundamental lack of love for each other. In that case, the priority may not be the worship meeting itself, but measures to deepen the common life of the congregation, such as meetings in informal groups for fellowship and prayer. Or the fundamental problem may be theological. The congregation simply may not understand the true nature of Christian worship, or may misunderstand the relationship between worship and the other aspects of congregational life. In that case, the priority may be teaching to rectify these misunderstandings. Or there may be deep problems in the personal lives of many members which stand in the way of deeper experience of the Lord. In that case, the priority may be pastoral care. Achievements in evangelism may result automatically in praise: if the angels worship over sinners who repent, what of the church?

Ideally, then, action by leaders to encourage more inspired worship in a congregation should form part of the leaders' general strategy for the strengthening of their congregations.

Praying and modelling

If there is truth in the traditional route to deeper worship, it is as it is applied to leaders and the mature Christians in a fellowship. It is they who need to ensure that they are personally prepared for worship, week by week. This is not simply a question of confession and personal experience of forgiveness, though it should certainly include that. It should include, too, the often-neglected ministry of earnest prayer that the Lord will reveal himself to the congregation as they worship together. Leaders need to strive in prayer for the protection and blessing of the congregation for which they are responsible.

It should also include waiting upon the Lord for the material, from scripture and in other ways, which can give the necessary lead to the congregation in worship and can set the spiritual tone in a truly spiritual way. It is an aspect of the false dichotomy which is often drawn between worship and the rest of life to hold that worship is only truly Spirit-led if the words come spontaneously within the particular worship event itself. Frequently, of course, the

Holy Spirit does greatly enrich worship by this means – it will be argued later that the Spirit should never be prevented from doing this. But, equally, to suggest that the Spirit cannot or does not lead in prior preparation is to place limitations on the Spirit which scripture implies he would decisively reject.

Not only should leaders themselves prepare, but they should teach and instruct all who have a part in leadership to prepare thoroughly themselves. This extends to worship leaders. It also includes musicians who have the dual tasks of technical and spiritual preparation. The latter should not be neglected for the benefit of the former. In worship, it is at least as important that the participants' spiritual credentials should be seen, as their intellectual and technical ones. For the same reason, the corporate preparation of those who lead in worship is important. Their spiritual unity and teamwork needs to be evident, as well as their technical teamwork.

Encouragement in worship should include the setting of good examples. If people are not to learn by painful experience, they must learn by observing others – and that is especially true in worship. Many people will never transcend the good or bad habits which they learn from their spiritual mentors. It is important, therefore, that those in leadership should seek to model the developments in worship which they believe the Lord wishes to see. If we exhibit narrow content, long empty silences, and a heavy religiosity which is not consistent with our manner in ordinary congregational life, it will not be surprising if those whom we disciple come to think that that is what worship ought to be like.

They will do so, of course, only for so long as they remain within our orbit. Increasingly, however, there is a mobility between areas, congregations, denominations and groups. People see other, more vibrant, dynamic and evidently spiritual modes of worship and, not surprisingly, they register their discontent with what they experience at home.

That points to the importance of leaders' being willing to learn from others. As opportunity arises in the course of travel, they should observe what is done in other congregations, in order to plunder shamelessly practices and approaches which might be profitable at home. They might even go as far as deliberately to seek out places where it is known that there is truly spiritual and spontaneous worship, in order to learn from those models.

Structuring worship

Paradoxical as it may seem, the quickest route to the restoration of spontaneity in worship may be to introduce some degree of structure, with the aim of helping people towards a deeper worship experience. In principle, the traditional 'Brethren' approach to 'open' worship confers the widest possible measure of freedom for participation, subject only to the possibility of intervention by the elders if contributions of a certain type, or by a particular individual, are persistently unacceptable because of their character, or theology, or the known unholy life of the participant.

This can present two problems. First, where worship has degenerated into a narrow and unacknowledged liturgy which is severely at odds with the principle, many present may simply feel that there is no point in trying to participate, since their contribution would either be falsely constrained or unacceptable.

Second, the very freedom inherent in the principle may be intimidating. For there are at least two ways of teaching people to swim. They may be invited simply to plunge in at the deep end and get on with it; or they may begin at the shallow end, with support from the teacher and other aids, and with *terra firma* close at hand. The first method is the more difficult! Yet, in worship, we often persist in asking people to launch out, with the thought in the back of their minds that the teacher will *not* plunge in and help if they get into difficulties, but criticise them from the poolside for their poor technique or simple incompetence.

It may be, therefore, that where open worship has become arid, an essential stepping stone for renewal may be for the leaders to introduce some degree of structure. For example, a specific president might be appointed whose task is to ensure that the period of worship is launched in a particular and helpful direction and who, prominently or discreetly, will seek under the leading of the Holy Spirit to steer the course of the whole event in a way which is spiritually rewarding. Such an individual might be an elder, or a teacher, or might be an instrumentalist or singer who has the necessary spiritual sensitivity and gifts. More widely, I recommend the formation of a worship band under appropriate leadership which draws widely on the musical skills of the congregation (see below).

Such leadership and structure can vary widely in character and degree. But, in my judgment, it is essential that the chief aim of the leader, and his or her supporters, should be to expand the horizons of the congregation in worship; in effect, both to model and teach worship. The aim should be to encourage the congregation's worship to the point at which individuals can be invited to take part spontaneously in a helpful way.

But, in the final analysis, the only criterion is whether the Lord is truly worshipped corporately. A completely unstructured event is of no value if the product is not true and spiritual worship, while a fully structured event will be biblical if the result is such worship (John 4:23–24).

Breaking moulds

In seeking renewal in worship, leaders may need considerable courage in addressing the existing structures of worship.

The traditional way of doing things at the Lord's table, as described earlier, may exercise a particularly powerful influence on the character of worship, both in style and content. Experience suggests that it can be very difficult to change the character of this event by a gradual process. It may be necessary in effect to bypass that meeting altogether, by creating a quite separate event in a congregation's programme which the leadership uses to encourage a quite different sort of worship. Alternatively, the mould may be broken by introducing a decisively different structure to the communion service. Either approach will require due Christian concern for those who are deeply attached, out of principle or habit, to the customary way of doing things. And, as with all changes which affect a voluntary group, much effort needs to be invested in preparing the group for the change and in gaining their assent.

Another tradition which leaders may need to seek to change is the endemic individualism of much that passes for Christian worship. Many come to worship with the notion that since, rightly, the purpose is the worship of God alone, the only thing that matters is what passes between themselves and God. This breeds a habit of mind in which the other people who have come together for the same purpose are mutually ignored. This attitude ignores the Lord's injunction that the true worshipper must first be reconciled with his brother and sister (Matt 5:23–24). It also ignores the New Testament emphasis on partnership in every aspect of the corporate life of the congregation, and the fact that communion is intended to be not only with the Lord but with the other members of the Christian body

(1 Cor 10: 1–22). Many coming to Christian worship, however, turn their backs mentally and emotionally on their fellow-worshippers to such an extent that they might as well be worshipping alone.

Where this is so, if a truly corporate worship is to be revived, leaders may need to seek to change attitudes by teaching by example, by structures, and by sensitive leading of worship, with the aim of obliging the congregation to recognize one another's presence. Appropriate ways include greeting one another, addressing one another at suitable moments, and acknowledging one another in passing the elements in communion. Such are the emotional hang-ups about intimacy, especially among the (?southern) English, that these steps may need to be taken with as great a sensitivity to the feelings of the group as those which affect the form and structure of the Breaking of Bread service.

Finding the right idiom

More widely, congregational leaders should seek an idiom of worship (music, poetry, words, style, etc) with which the particular congregation can identify and which they can make a satisfactory vehicle for their own worship of the Lord. Down the years, this has been both the source of hope and the cause of much frustration in Christian worship. One of the aspects of spiritual revival has always been that it tends to express itself in the musical and poetic idiom of the time. Luther purloined the popular tunes of his day. So did General William Booth, along with the uniform and military style of the jingoism of late Victorian England. Sankey adopted the popular musical expression of the 1860s, as can be seen by comparing his sacred songs with some of the marching tunes of the American Civil War. Now that those particular idioms have had their day, there is every reason for seeking to repeat the process in our times, provided that we are satisfied that there is no reason for rejecting a particular musical or poetic form as being unsuitable *in its very nature*.

This is to propose, however, a further assault upon tradition, in one of the most sacred areas of all. For, among the matters most likely to excite any traditionalist group of Christians, are two things: the hymnal from which they sing; and the time of the services!

It is also to suggest that the idiom of worship should be what is culturally popular. This, it must be recognized, presents a real difficulty for those of strong intellectual and aesthetic sensibilities, who often find the shallowness, banality and triviality of, in particular, popular worship songs difficult to stomach. This is not easy to handle. My natural sympathies are inclined to lie with the critics! But I believe that cultural elitism is bound to make worship inaccessible for the majority. The idiom of worship, for Christian and non-Christian alike, simply has to be popular – which does not mean that the popular has inevitably to be meretricious rather than meritorious!

Deepening content

Much of what passes for Christian worship is unsatisfactory because it is *spiritually* superficial, or focuses other than upon the God who is to be worshipped.

One remedy is to broaden and deepen the congregation's understanding of the material which is appropriate in worship. It is at this point that the traditional link between worship and the Lord's Supper as practised in 'Brethren' assemblies can be least helpful. A key feature of worship is an appreciation of who God is in all his limitless facets (see Rom 11: 33–36). Worship is, in essence, a *response* to God himself. It is often poverty-stricken because of a lack of appreciation and experience of God on the part of the congregation. In this respect, the narrowness already noted in the content is no help at all. If people are to worship corporately, it is essential that they should focus their mind from the beginning on the person of God and the magnitude of his works – of creation and of redemption.

It should not be assumed that the worshippers will necessarily arrive with appropriate material in their minds for this purpose. If they do not, then it is essential that the congregational leadership should ensure that the gap is repaired, by directing minds towards the Lord. This implies focusing upon the divine revelation of himself. The most obvious way to do this is through the reading and exposition of the word. That is why it has been so unfortunate that 'Brethren' tradition has tended to limit severely the forms of biblical contribution which have been considered appropriate in worship.

This biblical input can be provided in a variety of ways, of course. It may be that, contrary to the traditional form, worship should begin with pre-arranged expositional or devotional ministry rooted in scripture. So far as I am aware, there is no particular biblical warrant for the widespread practice of reserving the sermon to the end of any meeting. Indeed, some of the historic Christian liturgies place the word early rather than later in the order of service. Or, it may be that the leaders should simply adopt a policy of seeing that they themselves participate early in the worship period by reading and commenting on scripture, so as to inject material with which the congregation can begin to work and use as a launching pad for its worship. This will frequently be preferable to the time-honoured practice of taking up some phrase in the first hymn as the theme of worship.

Freeing for worship

But better leadership, more and better structures, and deeper theology will not, in my judgment, automatically produce a living congregational worship. If the spiritual input is confined to that of the worship leader, the congregation's experience of the Lord will get no further than his. It will be at the mercy of his or her state of mind, emotion and spirit at the particular time. Nor does it lie simply in better structures or in a formal liturgy which is of its very nature constricting (which is not to say that God cannot and does not use liturgical forms to great spiritual blessing sometimes). Nor does it lie in aesthetics, whether of language or music; nor in quality of performance in the worship service, whether by the worship leader or the preacher or musicians. Quality in these areas can be secured by human effort unaided by the Spirit. Nor, even, does it lie simply in deeper preaching of the word, though insofar as the Lord is revealed in his written word there should certainly be that response in the heart and life of the believer which constitutes worship.

Just as the whole purpose of teaching someone to swim or to ride a bicycle is to be able to stand back and watch them doing it for themselves, so the congregational leader's object must be to set the whole body free to worship as the Spirit leads them. One of the glories of the New Testament is that it reveals a priesthood for all believers, and the great object is that everyone at corporate worship should experience freedom to worship, audibly and inaudibly, the living God.

There are a number of areas in which freedom of form needs to be encouraged positively. Idiom has already been mentioned. Subject only to basic doctrinal checks, worshippers should be free to worship in the intellectual and emotional idiom in which they can best give expression to their thoughts and sentiments about the Lord. There should be a wide freedom as to content. Many subjects can be wholly conducive to worship, particularly where the focus is on the person, character and work of God (Father, Son and Holy Spirit – not just of Jesus as saviour).

In this context, it should be noted that too severe a requirement that the theme of a particular worship period should be respected can be very restrictive for many in a congregation. Such an approach can, in effect, limit audible contribution to those with the intellectual ability and knowledge, not to say ingenuity, to develop the particular theme. Others who might contribute very effectively to public worship may be intimidated into silence because they feel that they cannot develop the particular theme in an acceptable manner.

A wide variety of types of contribution should be perfectly acceptable. There is no reason, for example, why personal testimony of some recent experience of the Lord, or of what he has done for the individual concerned, should be regarded as inappropriate or embarrassing in worship. It should be made abundantly clear that short interventions are perfectly acceptable. Indeed, brief participation by a wide variety of people is perhaps the measure most likely to bring about more vibrant worship.

Freedom from unnecessary constraints of time may also be an important factor. It is interesting how bound congregations can become by the accustomed limits of their meetings. When the usual hour to finish has been reached, impatience to be away promptly begins to manifest itself. There may, on occasion, be legitimate practical reasons, of course. But often, when worship is burdensome, it is a symptom either of spiritual sluggishness or, perhaps, of the failure of the leadership to make the arrangements which set the congregation free to worship. By contrast, where there is spiritual revival, people show themselves to be quite unconcerned by the passage of time and are prepared to spend literally hours in prayer and praise – the events at Troas as recorded in Acts 20 were just the first recorded example of this phenomenon.

Sometimes a sufficient space of time is needed for a congregation to give proper expression to its corporate thoughts about the Lord, and the customary hour, up to half of which is taken up with preaching of some kind, is often simply not long enough. Some care and sensitivity to the feelings of the majority of the congregation are needed in making changes in this respect. The best course may be a gradual lengthening of the time allotted to worship, coupled with a policy of making it clear that at a certain point people are free to leave, but others may wish to continue in worship.

The structural integrity of spontaneous worship

Where worship is led by an individual or a group, and has been carefully prepared in advance, it is possible, whether by carnal or spiritual means, to achieve a satisfying coherence, balance and flow to different contributions. Once, however, the leader releases a meeting into free or spontaneous worship, these features may easily be lost. Worshippers need to be educated to the fact that they are not worshipping as individuals who are free to contribute just as they like. They need to be very conscious of one another, and responsive to what the Holy Spirit is saying and doing through others who are contributing. Congregational leaders, whether or not they are in charge of the particular occasion, need to be alert to this process and ready to contribute constructively themselves where it threatens to break down. They also need to stand ready to stimulate further thought, or to move the event on to a further stage in the cycle of worship, when that seems to be spiritually appropriate. If effective spontaneity is to be encouraged, the requirement is for worship leaders who are sympathetic to the leading of the Spirit in the gathering, and who can help the gathering to respond.

On the more practical side, congregations need to be educated in practices which are helpful to the flow of worship and those that are not. One feature which seems to me most unhelpful is unnecessary dependence upon the hymn-or songbook – a consequence, perhaps, of widespread literacy. It seems that congregations often cannot contemplate singing except from them. They bury their heads in them, even for pieces with which they have been totally familiar for many years, and the habit has developed of always waiting for the tune to be announced at length on the accompanying instrument. This can introduce quite unnecessary hiatus into worship, and reinforces the sense of individual isolation rather than the corporate nature of worship.

There are, of course, practical difficulties where numbers are small and musical expertise limited. But it would often be preferable for the coherence of worship if, under the leadership of the Spirit, an individual could take up a well-known song or hymn unannounced and the congregation could join in, if necessary unaccompanied. Then, either the accompanist(s) could transpose into the appropriate key, or, at a suitable opportunity, shift the key appropriately. Even where songbooks are available, it often helps to display the pieces on an overhead projector in order to lift the heads of the congregation and to enable them to be more conscious of the corporate nature of worship. (This implies, of course, that questions of copyright must be properly attended to, and that arrangements be made for operating the projector and looking after the slides.)

Those presiding at worship should not neglect silence in worship, either. It is not the case that all silences are empty. It may be very helpful, from time to time, positively to encourage everyone present to worship the Lord silently for a period – though it is wise to make sure that they have the material ready to mind with which to do this.

Identifying and encouraging spiritual gifts

The whole point of open or spontaneous worship is to give opportunity for the exercise of the diverse spiritual gifts which are available in the particular gathering. It follows, therefore, that leaders should be seeking to identify those who have such gifts and encouraging them to develop and exercise them for the benefit of the body as a whole. By contrast, it will not help much if participation is dominated by those who are not suitably gifted.

There are some spiritual gifts which are obviously of particular relevance to worship. If it is held that the full range of spiritual gifts is still available to the church and there is no restriction on their use, then Paul refers in 1 Corinthians 14 to six which are clearly relevant: prophecy; knowledge; revelation; teaching; tongues (ecstatic utterances); and interpretation of tongues. He also refers to contributing a hymn, possibly spontaneously composed under spiritual inspiration (v 26)[1]. The reference to knowledge suggests that utterance of wisdom and utterance of knowledge, mentioned in 1 Corinthians 12:8, are also relevant.

Prophecy and revelation are clearly of especial importance, if only because Paul says so explicitly: 'If all prophesy, and an unbeliever

---

1. So C K Barrett: 'A fresh, perhaps spontaneous, composition, not an Old Testament psalm, is intended' (*A Commentary on the First Epistle to the Corinthians*, second edition, 1971, 327).

or outsider enters, he is convicted by all. . . the secrets of his heart are disclosed; and so falling on his face, he will worship God and declare that God is really among you' (1 Cor 14:2–25). What is true for the unbeliever seems to be likely to be even more true for the believer.

For the English, the almost automatic principal connotation of prophecy is with foretelling future events. Some prophecy in the New Testament undoubtedly had that character, as when Agabus foretold extensive famine (Acts 11:27–28) and the imprisonment of Paul (Acts 21:1–11), the latter apparently in confirmation of numerous such prophecies elsewhere ('the Holy Spirit testifies to me in every city that imprisonment and afflictions await me' – Acts 20:23; see also Rev 22:6). But, in the New Testament, the main burden of the concept of prophecy lies elsewhere: in giving direct instructions to a congregation (Acts 13:1–2), in exhorting and strengthening it (Acts 15:32), and in building it up and consoling it (1 Cor 14:3). In referring to 'some revelation or knowledge or prophecy or teaching' (1 Cor 14:6), Paul may have in mind a spectrum stretching from a reminder of established and general Christian truth on the one hand, to a more directly intended word from God to the particular congregation on the other.

Many, of course, baulk at the idea that God still speaks directly today in congregational worship, but it is not clear why the idea should present such difficulty. It may be argued that the whole point of worship is to enter the presence of God and to experience him. If pre-Christian people heard him, it must be even more the case that those in the Christian era should hear him (see, for example, Isaiah 6 where God speaks directly; Luke 1:8–20 where he speaks through the angel; and 2 Chronicles 5–7 where he speaks both directly and through Solomon to the people in prophetic mode). Evangelical Christians have long held that God speaks directly to individual Christians in conversion and subsequently in order to guide them. It is not clear why he should be prohibited from doing this to the congregation as a whole as it meets together.

They have long held, too, that he speaks directly through the exposition of scripture and the preaching of the gospel. But it is not obvious why he should now have confined himself to those methods of communication to a congregation. Such communication will, of course, be consistent with God's authoritative revelation of himself in the scripture – which is presumably the main reason why the prophets were required to test the utterances of their brethren (1 Cor 14.29–32; 1 Thess 5:20–21; and 1 John 4:1). But there is an obvious distinction to be drawn between revelation which purports to add to God's general enduring revelation of himself to the church as encapsulated in the scriptures, and revelation which deals with the specifics of the life and ministry of an individual or of a congregation, and which for that reason is limited in time and place.

The conclusion is that, without exercise of the intelligible gifts which Paul enumerates in 1 Corinthians 14, worship is likely to be comparatively impoverished. Their exercise is clearly related to the importance of deepening the spiritual content of worship from the word, as already mentioned. This is a vital area in which congregational leaders need to encourage the exercise of gift, if worship is to be enriched and freed into effective spontaneity.

This is an issue, however, on which more needs to be said from the practical point of view – because regrettably, it is an area in which the elders of 'Brethren' assemblies are, by virtue of inexperience, often poorly equipped to give a positive lead. The difficulty does not, of course, arise with respect to prayer, scripture reading, and exhortation, all of which are familiar enough activities within the tradition. But it does arise with respect to, for example, prophecy, revelation, utterance of knowledge and wisdom, tongues, and interpretation, and indeed simple matters like praying for others in a helpful way.

There is a danger of a 'Charismatic' mystique on these matters: that only those who have a special unction or experience can understand what is being referred to – with the result that those who lack it are disqualified, or feel themselves disqualified, from giving leadership in these matters. It would help for leaders who want to encourage the use of the full range of relevant gifts in worship to go out of their way to learn something about the neglected gifts, by visiting places where it is purported that they are used, talking to leaders who have such experience, reading, etc. But leaderships should also seek the Lord in prayer that the full range of gifts will be manifest in their congregations, and they should also make it clear that the exercise of the full range is acceptable.

They will also need procedures for judging gifts. If prophecy, or interpretation, or knowledge is claimed, they need to be sure that the claims are justified and, if they have doubts, to take appropriate steps. This demands spiritual discernment on their own part as elders and leaders, which they need earnestly to seek from the Lord. It also requires the courage to exercise control where necessary.

Identifying and encouraging natural gifts

It is not disembodied spirits who come to worship God, but whole human beings. Our Lord's injunction is: 'You shall love the Lord your God with all your heart, and with all your soul, and with all your mind, and with all your strength' (Mark 12:30 – the last term generally refers to physical strength). In the Judaeo-Christian understanding it is difficult to draw meaningful distinctions between body, mind and spirit. Where there is true worship, therefore, it is only to be expected that it will find legitimate expression in the mind, the emotions and even physically. So there is much that can be done to enrich worship by encouraging the use of the natural gifts with which the group is endowed – instrumental, vocal, poetic.

This can be done in a way which also encourages freedom and spontaneity in worship. There is no law, for example, which says that the instrumental accompaniment of Christian worship should be limited to one instrument, any more than there was once a law in' Brethren' assemblies which limited it to none. There are many congregations elsewhere in the world where all instrumentalists are encouraged to bring their instrumental gift to worship as naturally as, traditionally, the gift of teaching has been brought to worship in 'Brethren' churches.

Provided that the overall result is orderly and edifying, there is no need to be too concerned about musical balance. Congregational singing will, in any case, to a large extent mask that, and many churches are discovering that accompaniment by a small musical group is more helpful in worship than that of a single rather inflexible instrument. Some instruments do seem more flexible than others in accompaniment of spontaneous worship. And instrumentalists who can accurately recall and pitch tunes by ear are particularly valuable in assisting congregations to worship without unnecessary interruption. They should be strongly encouraged to help in freeing worship.

Vocalists, also, need to be encouraged to use their skills, both collectively in giving a strong lead to congregational singing, and in making spontaneous individual contributions in song. Here, congregations, and especially worship leaders, need to be alert to whether or not the vocalist should be left to contribute individually, and to when the congregation should be encouraged to join in. The possibility of instrumental solos should not be neglected either; for example, during periods of silent worship or when the elements are passing from one to another.

One aspect of gift which generally tends to be neglected is that of the lyric writer and poet. Where the Holy Spirit is really at work in a congregation, it is to be expected that people will not confine themselves exclusively to the literary vehicles of worship which have been provided by former generations, or from people outside the congregation. Where there is genuine spiritual experience combined with lyrical gift, it should be natural for the individuals concerned to give expression to their praises in original work. The rest of the congregation should, in turn, be pleased to take up such work themselves as expressions which stem from their common experience.

That it seems so rare may be because of want of deep contemporary spiritual experience. But it may also be because the individuals concerned have not been trained to see it as a possible way of expressing their praises and rendering useful service to the Body of Christ. Congregational leaders may also have failed themselves to see the possibilities in this area and to encourage the exercise of the relevant gifts. In either case, it would follow that the congregation is the poorer because gift is not being exercised 'for the common good' (1 Cor 12:7). For myself, I do not see why, in addition to instrumental, vocal and lyrical gifts, the rhythmic gifts of dance should not be deployed in congregational worship from time to time; though I grant that care should be taken, out of concern for the conscience of the weaker brother and sister.

In the use of this type of gift, I believe, too, that there should be room for the air or lyric which is spontaneously composed at the time of worship under the guidance of the Holy Spirit. If any of this should seem strange or shocking, I would say only that they seem to me to be possibilities which are implicit in the principles of spontaneous worship as pioneered by the early 'Brethren' (among other groups). It is surely not to be supposed that the full possibilities were revealed to them. They were children of their times, and past and familiar practice was bound to limit their understanding – as it will ours. Often in spiritual practice, it will be for us, under the guidance of the Spirit, to take up the trail from the point reached by others.

In encouraging the exercise of these gifts, congregational leaders should be careful to enjoin on the people concerned a number of important principles.

First, they need to understand the need to refine and develop their particular gifts for the benefit of the congregation, just as the teacher needs to prepare himself spiritually and technically (1 Tim 4:1–15). In the case of a musical ensemble this implies collective preparation as well as individual preparation.

Second, as already noted, it is not simply a matter of technical proficiency. Spiritual preparation is important, and adequate time needs to be given to worship as well as practice.

Third, and most important, instrumentalists, vocalists and lyricists *must* understand clearly that their task in worship is not to *perform* to the congregation. It is, rather, both to lead and help the assembled company as a whole to worship before the throne of God. It follows, therefore, that the hearts and minds of musicians and singers should be directed towards the Lord, rather than towards the congregation. ('It was the duty of the trumpeters and singers to make themselves heard in unison in praise and thanksgiving to the LORD'– 2 Chron 5:13.) This is often a hard lesson for musicians to learn who have been brought up in the post-Enlightenment tradition of musical performance *to* others.

Fourth, there is the point of the subtle relation between musicians and the rest of the congregation. The task is not to accompany or to follow; it is to lead and help. There are many congregations whose worship is impaired, either because musicians will not shoulder properly the responsibility of leading song, or because they dominate the proceedings to such an extent that it becomes a struggle between them and the rest of the congregation. Where, however, the ministry is properly exercised, there are great benefits in prospect: in Solomon's temple, it was the presence of the glory of God (2 Chron 5:13–14).

Blending spiritual gifts in leading worship

'When you come together, each one has a hymn, a lesson, a revelation, a tongue, or an interpretation. Let all things be done for edification.' The purpose of the exercise of spiritual gifts is to build up (1 Cor 14:3, 26), for the common good, as just noted, and finally to express unity (1 Cor 12:12; see also Eph 4: 3–6, 16). It follows, therefore, that, the multiple exercise of gift notwithstanding, worship should amount to a satisfying unity, expressing the unity of the Spirit with the Father and the Son (John 17:1–26). Free or spontaneous worship should not be a series of disparate contributions; if it is, it calls into question the reality of what is claimed to be taking place. A special burden rests with those who lead worship, with those who lead singing, with musicians and singers, and everyone else who takes part prominently, to give expression to that unity.

To achieve that, they need to be especially conscious of the leading of the Holy Spirit not only within themselves, but in each other and in the gathering as a whole. It calls for teamwork in which, under God, they seek to blend their various gifts for the benefit of the whole. They must be prepared to respond to each other's leadership. The president or the principal leader must be ready to give place to another who believes that he or she has, from the Lord, something which is critically necessary to the gathering at that particular point. Especially, worship leaders and musicians need to seek to blend their contributions to give a clear and flowing lead to the gathering as a whole.

CONCLUSION

'O the depth of the riches and wisdom and knowledge of God. How unsearchable are his judgements and how inscrutable his ways. "For who has known the mind of the Lord, or who has been his counsellor?" "Or who has given a gift to him that he might be repaid?" For from him and through him and to him are all things. To him be glory for ever. Amen.'(Rom 11:33–36) If the object of worship is to experience the presence of this God, we cannot expect that it will be possible to tie him down with formularies on the one hand, or with particular methods, techniques and practices on the other. He will reveal himself as he chooses. Regrettably, it is always possible to manufacture in the energy of the flesh something that will pass, even among Christians, for true Christian worship. Moreover, it may not be wise simply to try to copy what other Christians do. For them, they may be worshipping in spirit and in truth. For us the same arrangements and practices may simply be a counterfeit. Quite apart from principle, this may simply be a matter of practicality. For example, what is appropriate in a gathering of 200 or 1,000 worshipping Christians may not be at all relevant or practicable in a gathering of 20. Within the general framework of scriptural teaching on worship, it is for the individual gathering to seek to use the gifts among it so as to give authentic expression to the worship of God.

If scripture is viewed as a whole, it becomes clear that corporate worship and individual prayer can take many different outward forms, varying with place, time and culture. It is the object of worship which is of abiding importance: to experience the Lord in reality and to respond to him in adoration and commitment, with all that that implies. Happily, we have numerous models in scripture which indicate for us something of the character of true worship, for example, in the Psalms, in passages in the prophets like Isaiah 12 and Ezekiel 1, and in the book of Revelation. Our task is to seek that authentic experience of the Lord in our own congregation. We must wait upon the Lord for this experience of himself. But it is my conviction that we do not need to lie idly on the hillside like the poet waiting for the muse. In Christian thinking, seeking is a more active mode than that. As I have suggested, there is much that congregational leaders can and should do to help the Christian community in the quest.

4

The breaking of bread: a meal with meaning

Alan G Palmer

Alan has exercised a pastoral ministry in churches in Canada and England. He has also served as director of the Open Learning Centre of Oak Hill College, London. This essay is based on a chapter of his M Th thesis.

INTRODUCTION

'Wonderful things in the Bible I see; some put there by you, and some by me.'As we approach the various issues raised in this chapter it is vital that we recognise that we come to them with personal presuppositions. It is becoming increasingly recognised that *anyone* coming to the text of scripture brings with them their own preconceived ideas. As Graham Stanton has noted, an individual's presuppositions 'are involved in every aspect of the relationship of the interpretation of his text'.[1] Writing about worship in general, David Petersen states: 'Even those who desire to bring their theology and practice under the criticism and control of the biblical revelation can find themselves in serious conflict with one another. Most of us are more conditioned by custom and personal preference than we would care to admit.'[2]

The presuppositions that we all hold must be recognised as our 'pre-understanding', which can be either a help or a hindrance to every aspect of understanding the biblical text or to the process of theological reflection. If our pre-understanding is not flexible and does not allow for change and modification to both our theoretical

---

1. In I H Marshall, ed, *New Testament Interpretation*, Paternoster, 1997, 61.
2. D Petersen, *Engaging with God*, Apollos, 1.

and applied theology, then we will go no further than our presuppositions will allow. Stanton recognises this when he writes: 'If an individual's prejudice is so deep seated that, in effect, a verdict is passed before the evidence is even considered, then surely, prejudice negates the possibility of understanding a text.' (op cit, 62) We might add that deep-seated prejudice will prevent new ways of thinking theologically and hinder attempts at innovative practice.

THE BREAKING OF BREAD (THE LORD'S SUPPER)[1]

Bearing our presuppositions in mind, we will attempt to 'revisit' the biblical texts that have informed the approach of the 'Brethren' to the Lord's Supper. We shall not ignore the two thousand years of church history, or the one hundred and sixty years of 'Brethren' history. However we will try to engage in 'a critical re-reading of the foundational documents in the belief that this is a way to critique and challenge contemporary practice.'[2]

Setting the scene

Without 1 Corinthians 10:16–17 and 11:17–34 we would know virtually nothing about how the Lord's Supper was celebrated in New Testament times. Ironically, therefore, we should be grateful to the Corinthians for their abuses, since without them we would not have Paul's corrective and informative response.

The abuses at the Lord's Supper posed a very serious problem for Paul and his informants, but not, it would appear, for the Corinthians. They had indeed written to the apostle asking his advice on a number of important issues (see 1 Cor 7:1 etc), but the Lord's Supper was not one of them. Evidently they did not think it to be of vital importance, even though it was causing factions among them (1 Cor 11:18–19). James Dunn writes:

> Evidently the unity of the Corinthian church was most at risk precisely because the expression of unity and mutual sharing (1 Cor 10:16–17) had become an expression of greed and incon-

---

1. We will use the term 'Lord's Supper' for the most part because this is how the Breaking of Bread is referred to in most commentaries and articles.
2. D Horrell, *Theology*, May/June 1995, 197.

siderateness (1 Cor 11:21). Ironically the focus of unity had become the focus of division – an irony often repeated in the history of Christianity.[1]

Understanding the Lord's Supper

There has been much debate over the exact background to the Lord's Supper. The apparent parallel between the sacrificial meals of Israel and contemporary cults (see 1 Cor 10:18–21) invited exploration of the idea that the Christian sacrament had been decisively influenced by the cultic meals of pagan mysteries.[2] The very fact that Eleusis, where the famous mysteries were celebrated, was only fourteen miles from Corinth, suggests a connection. However, Dunn wisely concludes:

> Since we know so little about the mysteries and their meals (they kept their secret well), since eating has always been such a common focus of community, and since the rationale of the Lord's Supper seems to be quite fully enough explicated from the tradition of the Lord's Supper inherited by Paul in and from the earliest days of the new movement, we need hardly look further for explanation of the practices of the Pauline churches (op cit, 77).

More recently, attempts have been made to locate the background to the Lord's Supper more securely in the Jewish tradition of Passover meals. From the fact that the Passover meal begins with breaking bread and ends with the cup 'after supper' (1 Cor 11:25) it has been concluded that the Lord's Supper was itself a meal with the bread and wine beginning and completing it.

Archaeology informs us that the homes which acted as the early Christians' meeting places were of limited size. These 'meals', then, were not large affairs and appear to have been part of everyday life, yet expressing a deep sense of identity and community.

What was the problem at Corinth?

'Social stratification' may have been the basis of the Corinthian problems at the Lord's Supper. The richer members of the Corinthian congregation, who hosted these meals, seem to have been

1. *1 Corinthians*, Sheffield Academic Press, 1995, 76.
2. See G Fee, *The First Epistle to the Corinthians*, Eerdmans, 1987, 531.

abusing their position of privilege. It appears that they were 'going ahead' (Gk *prolambanei*) and eating their meals, leaving little for the poorer members who arrived later (1 Cor 11:21). In this way, the rich Christians were humiliating the poorer believers. This was something that Paul could not tolerate (1 Cor 11:22).

Scholars suggest several forms that this humiliating practice could have taken. Some, for example, believe that the richer Christians were served better portions of food, ie, better quality than the poorer attenders. This was simply in line with the Greco-Roman etiquette of the time. One served one's social equal with the best quality foods and the poorer guests received what was left.

Others have suggested that the problem at Corinth was that some came early and began eating before the others arrived. The late-comers, probably slaves or poorer freemen and women, did not have enough time or money to prepare food for themselves. Arriving late, they would find most of the expensive food brought by the wealthier early-comers already eaten. Also, late-comers might well find that there was insufficient room in the 'dining room' (*triclinium*) and would have to sit outside in the *atrium*.

The idea that 'social ranking' was going on in Corinth is picked up and amplified by others. They note that to rank one's guests in terms of social status was a common practice. The problem was that the Corinthians were following the social conventions of their time and treating the Lord's Supper just like any other banquet. Paul does not tell the Corinthians not to have meals together at all. He encourages them to make a distinction between the private meals in one's home and shared meals in the *ecclesia*, no matter whose home it is held in. For Paul this is a matter, not of a sacred space, but of a sacred time and occasion.

How does Paul respond to the problem?

In the light of this 'social stratification', Paul has no commendation for the Corinthians (1 Cor 11:17). He recognises that there are indeed (social?) schisms and factions among them. Those fractious individuals help to hilight the more genuine members of the congregation (1 Cor 11:18–19). As we have noted, however, the apostle does not rule out these meals altogether. No, his concern is to point out that pagan rules of protocol do not apply when one meets at the Lord's table (see 1 Cor 11:20–22).

The apostle is trying to restore a sense of 'democracy' among the Corinthian Christians. He wants to underline the fact that social status counts for nothing at the Lord's Supper. To help reinforce this egalitarian approach, Paul goes back to the institution of the Lord's Supper (1 Cor 11:23–26). This meal with his disciples prefigured the cross on which Christ would die to bring about equality among his followers (see 1 Cor 12:13; Gal 3:27). The Corinthians needed to be reminded of this, and so Paul chooses his words carefully to bring about the desired effect. Notice how he uses the 'technical language of Judaism'. Barrett notes that, 'The language is the language of tradition in the technical sense, and corresponds to that which had been established in Judaism.' 'Received' (*parelabon*) corresponds to the Hebrew *qibbel* and 'handed/passed on' (*paredoka*) to *masar*.[1]

We have here an account which stands as the earliest record of what happened at the Last Supper. Indeed, as Morris notes, 'it is the earliest record of any words of our Lord'.[2] Also, the apostle appears to be claiming a direct revelation: 'I received from the Lord' (1 Cor 11:23). Morris considers that we should take this as it stands because 'there are several other references to revelations made directly to Paul'. (See Acts 18:9f; 22:18; 23:11; 27:23–25; Gal 1:12; 2:2; 2 Cor 12:7, and Morris, op cit, 159.) However, this should not prevent us from recognising that Paul also had access to other traditions. The apostle then, is passing on to the Corinthians a tradition that is vivid in his memory.

It has been suggested that the Corinthians may have been viewing the Lord's Supper as a funerary meal, one where a dead hero was remembered. However, the tradition, as Paul records it, shows that what Jesus did at the Last Supper was not to institute a funerary rite. The word 'new' (1 Cor 11:25) is fatal to the view that the words of Jesus recorded here in 1 Corinthians 11 :24f were intended to be his last will and testament. *Diatheke* is, rather, a reference to the founding of a New Covenant relationship (where all are equal), by Christ's death (see Jer 31:33–34). The apostle wants the Corinthians to be aware that the remembering (*anamnesis* means 'the activity of calling to mind') that occurs at the Lord's Supper is not an occasional, perhaps annual, memorial service for Jesus. It is both a vivid

---

1. C K Barrett, op cit, 264–265.
2. Leon Morris, *The First Epistle of Paul to the Corinthians*, Tyndale, 1958, 159.

recollection and a vigorous proclamation of what Christ's death and resurrection have achieved.

Leon Morris notes that 'proclaim' (1 Cor 11:26) should not be rendered 'present' in the sense of 'presenting Christ to God' in the Lord's Supper. He states that, in the New Testament, 'proclaim' (*katangello*) is used mostly of preaching the gospel. 'Always it denotes an activity exercised towards men, and never one exercised towards God' (op cit, 162). According to Paul then, the Lord's Supper is an opportunity to proclaim to believers and unbelievers the results and benefits of the cross, and to do this 'until he [Christ] comes' (1 Cor 11:26).

While the Lord's Supper may be derived in some sense from the Passover meal, it stands out from the Passover. Admittedly, Jesus did break the bread after giving thanks (1 Cor 11:24), but this does not prove he was celebrating a Passover meal, since thanksgiving over bread was part of every Jewish meal.[1] What he was probably doing was to modify the Passover traditions.

We need to point out here that the tradition, as cited by Paul, does not associate the breaking of the bread with the breaking of Jesus' body. The Supper is not a re-enactment of the Passion (no bones of Jesus were broken). In a similar way, Paul does not specifically link the cup to Jesus' blood, but calls it 'the cup of the new covenant' (1 Cor 11:25). The Lord did not ask his disciples to drink blood, something to which Jews would react with horror. Accordingly, the apostle says nothing about wine representing Christ's blood. (See the Markan version, Mk 14:24.)

In the context of our wider discussion and the question of 'What happens to the sacraments at the Lord's Supper?', we should note that Paul is silent on this issue.

We have already noted that the apostle stresses that the celebration of the Supper entails, not only eating and drinking, but also the proclamation of Christ's death until his return (1 Cor 11:26). In this way, the Supper considers the past, present and the future. A number of scholars suggest that the Aramaic phrase *mara natha*, which means 'Our Lord come', was an integral part of the Lord's Supper for early Jewish Christians. The mention of the 'Lord's coming' appears to prepare the way for the discussion of judgment in 1 Corinthians 11:27–32.

---

1. J Jeremias, *The Eucharistic Words of Jesus*, SCM, 1966, 15ff.

In his discussion, Paul seems to be referring to the actual crucified body of Christ, as the reference to 'blood' appears to make clear. Indeed, the 'old way' of viewing this was that Paul was referring to the bread and the wine. However, and in keeping with our argument that 'social stratification' was the problem at Corinth, perhaps we should approach the text in a different way. We believe that the mention of 'unworthy' here refers not to unworthy people – after all we are all unworthy – but to unworthy practices. This would fit well into our reasoning that the examination called for in 1 Corinthians 11:28 is to one's consideration of how properly to participate in the Lord's Supper, not a morbid introspective assessment of one's worthiness to take part.

There were, then, some among the Corinthian congregation who were abusing the Lord's Supper and thereby partaking in an unworthy manner. They were guilty in some sense of the 'body and blood of Christ'. They were taking part without 'discerning the body (1 Cor 11:29). We believe that, while 'the body' here might refer to Christ's death, which was ironically being forgotten in the midst of eating the meal, it is more likely that Paul was referring to believers as 'the body of Christ'. Some members of the Corinthian congregation were eating without taking their fellow believers into account, ie, they were eating 'inappropriately'. Once again, this view fits well into our 'social stratification' hypothesis. Richer Christians were humiliating poorer Christians by way of social segregation at the Lord's Supper. They were, in some sense, guilty of siding with those who abused and executed Christ. In future, Paul wants them to share the Lord's Supper with their brothers and sisters as one body in Christ, rather than following pagan protocol.

The apostle makes clear the serious nature of the situation at Corinth when he speaks in terms of 'judgment'. The Corinthians were liable to bring temporal or, possibly, eternal judgment upon themselves if they did not alter their behaviour (1 Cor 11:29). Signs of this were already present, some being sick and others having died (1 Cor 11:30) – and there was a severe famine in AD 53 which may well have added extra emphasis to Paul's words. This disaster, however, could have been avoided. If the Corinthians had changed their ways, then the illnesses and deaths would have achieved their tasks of preventing further judgment (1 Cor 11:31–32). It seems likely that Paul viewed these temporal judgments as remedial or disciplinary in character, rather than final.

Some scholars understand 'wait for' (*ekdechesthe*, 1 Cor 11:33a) as an encouragement for the Corinthians to 'wait to' eat with the late-comers. However, in the context where 'social elitism' was a problem, it is probably better to understand *ekdeschesthe* as 'welcome' or 'receive one another'. The Corinthians, then, were 'to welcome' one another in the sense that all would partake together, without distinctions in rank or food. The point of the Lord's Supper is not to satisfy hunger, and so it must not be treated as just another banquet (1 Cor 11:34).

In concluding this section, we note Dunn's words that, 'it can hardly be doubted that the problems in the Corinthian assembly were caused not by theological disagreement but by social status and convention running counter to the more egalitarian ethos of Pauline Christianity' (op cit, 79). In the apostle's view, the sacred tradition concerning the Lord's Supper is recited (1 Cor 11:23–26) specifically to encourage social levelling, to overcome the factionalism created by stratification and its expression at meals, and to create unity and harmony in the congregation.

The Lord's Supper, liturgy and worship

Before going on to discuss the practical implications of the theology of the Lord's Supper, we need to clarify some important issues. The first of these concerns the basis of the 'Brethren' style of observing the Lord's Supper. We know that, like many churches, the 'Brethren' do not celebrate it as a 'full meal'. They have simply retained the bread and the wine as the 'essential elements'. However, having said this, we still need to ask the question: Was a form of 'worship service' attached to the Lord's Supper in the Early Church? The 'Brethren' liturgical form is based on an affirmative answer to this question.

We must therefore examine the evidence for such a structure in the New Testament. Paul's first letter to the Corinthians may help us here. With 1 Corinthians 11 we seem to have finished with the Lord's Supper. However, the next three chapters are still concerned with the Corinthian assembly, even though Paul is mainly concerned with the balanced use of 'spiritual gifts', ie, prophecy, tongues etc. But to return to the case in point, is there evidence that the Corinthian assembly had one (weekly) meeting, or did they have two; one for the Lord's Supper and another for instruction and the exercise of spiritual gifts?

A good case has been made for one weekly meeting including both the Lord's Supper and a time of worship with the use of spiritual gifts. Hickling suggests that it may have been difficult or impossible to hold two plenary sessions a week, and that, in 1 Corinthians 11; 12–14, Paul is describing two aspects or phases of the one assembly.[1]

When we review the Corinthian material, we discover that there is indeed a notable continuity between 1 Corinthians 11 and 12–14. This is particularly the case in Paul's elaboration of the 'body image' of 1 Corinthians 10:16,17, which he takes up in 1 Corinthians 11:23,24,29,33, and applies to the 'diversity-in-unity' of the Christian fellowship in 1 Corinthians 12:12–30. There is good evidence, then, from Paul's letter to the Corinthian congregation that they, at least, had a combined Lord's Supper and worship service where spiritual gifts were exercised and instruction took place.

The role of elders

One more issue remains for us to deal with before we move on. Who presided at these meetings? We know that church leadership had become more clearly defined by the time the Pastoral Letters were written. We also know that there is evidence in the *Didache* (circa 100 AD) of presidency at the Lord's Supper. However, Paul makes no overt mention of who is to administer the elements or who is to enact the discipline laid down in 1 Corinthians 14:27–33.

On Jewish precedents, the father or 'elder' of the house would have said the opening blessing over the bread; the thanksgiving over the cup, according to later Jewish evidence, could be delegated to a privileged guest. Hickling suggests that 'perhaps all was in the hands of Paul's special agents in Corinth (1 Cor 16:15f) to whom obedience was expected (op cit, 194).

However, there is an alternative to this viewpoint. It may be the case that the leadership of the Corinthian assembly was in the hands of those whom the New Testament terms 'elders'. Although Paul does not mention them in this context, we do know that he recognised their value in other churches. (See Acts 20:13–18; 1 Tim 3:1–13; Titus 1:5–9.) The model for this kind of church leadership may well

---

1. J A Hickling, *The Study of Liturgy*, eds C Jones, G Wainwright, E Yarnold and P Bradshaw, SPCK, 1993, 93.

have been taken from a Jewish context where 'elders' were recognised in terms, not of status, but of 'age and wisdom'. Dr Alastair Campbell affirms that elders, 'refers collectively to men who were individually overseers of the churches that met in their homes. Each person is an overseer and together they are the Seniors', ie, elders.[1]

If this is the case, then the 'Brethren' may be right to emphasise the need of 'overseeing elders in their assemblies'[2], but mistaken in their insistence on 'no human leadership' at their Breaking of Bread services. For it seems clear that Paul expected there to be responsible leadership in these meetings to maintain decency and order (1 Cor 14:26–29.[3]

Liturgy of the Lord's Supper

Let us briefly examine the 'liturgy' that the 'Brethren' have drawn from 1 Corinthians 14:26–39. We should first note that they have reversed the order that is present in the Corinthian letter. There, the (meal) and the sacrament appear to have preceded the open worship. Among the 'Open Brethren' the open worship comes first and is then followed by the sacrament.

The 'Brethren' appear to have tried to keep the informal format of the Corinthian worship time, ie, 'everyone has a hymn, or a word of instruction, a revelation' (1 Cor 14:26f), but they have largely rejected the 'charismatic' aspects of 'tongues' and 'inspired prophetic speech'. This negative reaction to the charismatic gifts of tongues and prophecy is largely historical in origin. Darby's rejection of the Irvingite teaching on these gifts has left a lasting impression not only on the 'Brethren' but also on a number of Evangelical Free Church traditions.[4] 'Brethren' writers, like Bland, were fiercely cessationist and the contemporary Canadian 'Brethren' author, John Williams, still holds this traditional stance to these gifts.[5]

Two points of application can be made here. First, we would encourage a re-examination of the evidence for 'charismatic worship' in the light of 1 Corinthians 14:26–39. There is still a need for

1. A Campbell, *The Elders. Seniority within Earliest Christianity*, T&T Clark, 1994, 13.
2. A G Palmer, *The Servant Leader*, Unpublished Master's Thesis, Regent College, Vancouver, 1984, 1–10.
3. See D A Carson, *Showing the Spirit*, Baker, 1987, 134.
4. See J N Darby, *Collected Writings. Apologetics*, vol 4, ed W Kelly, 444–445; T C F Stunt, *Christian Brethren Research Fellowship Journal*, Dec 1965, 40–48.
5. F C Bland, *The Witness*, May 1926, 322; J Williams, *The Holy Spirit*, Loizeau, New Jersey, 1980, 205.

simplicity and supernaturalism within the assemblies, and this has biblical warrant. The 'Brethren' fear that 'charismatic worship' may well lead to disorder needs to be addressed, for again this is a biblical concern. Carson comments on 1 Corinthians 14:33a: 'This truth does not of course sanction mere traditionalism in worship, or sanctify stuffiness; but it does warn us sharply about the dangers of the opposite end of the spectrum.' (op cit, 21) However, many churches would benefit from a re-evaluation of the role of the Holy Spirit in open worship. The 'giving gift' of the Spirit's nature has been largely underemphasised and undervalued.[1]

The second point of application appears to contradict the first, but it is more a question of maintaining balance. There is a need to continue to learn to balance 'spontaneity' with 'planning and structure'. The Spirit is capable of inspiring pre-planned services, written prayers and orchestrated music and drama. This kind of pre-planning may well result in more individuals being involved in the 'open worship' and may help prevent the peril of 'predictable spontaneity'.

LITURGY AND THE LIFE OF THE COMMUNITY

We recognise that the 'Brethren' in general have reacted vehemently against the idea of a 'liturgy' being followed in the Breaking of Bread service. Perhaps this is because they have understood liturgy as an 'ecclesiastical structure'; something 'imposed' on the congregation which threatens their spiritual liberty. It may help to view liturgy, instead, as a 'species of significant human behaviour'.[2] What a particular group of Christians repeatedly do when they gather for worship, what they see as significant behaviour, helps to define their liturgy. So the 'Brethren' find their 'ecclesiastical identity' in the manner in which they celebrate the Lord's Supper.

The 'Brethren' have rightly placed the cross at the centre of their Breaking of Bread liturgy, and they are not alone in this.[3] However, we believe that the true significance of this has not been fully realised. If the cross is at the centre of what the 'Brethren' believe to be the central meeting of the church, then it should have significant

---

1. T Smail, *The Giving Gift: The Holy Spirit in Person*, DLT, 1994, 15–17.
2. M Searle, *The Study of Liturgy*, eds C Jones et al, SPCK, 1993, 52.
3. J R W Stott, *The Cross of Christ*, IVP, 1986, 273.

repercussions for individual Christian communities. The liturgy of the Breaking of Bread service, with its focus on the cross, should affect everything that Christians do. For liturgy is our 'work' for God and for his people.

The cross spells the end to all barriers of race, religion, social position and gender distinction (Gal 3:27–28). Now we have a common commitment and a common memory. We are a 'Catholic Community' because, as Zizioulas writes, 'the ultimate essence of catholicity lies in the transcendence of all divisions in Christ'.[1] In the light of this, congregations may wish to re-evaluate their understanding of issues such as the following.

The role of women

The 'Brethren' have traditionally taught the submission and silence of women in mixed gatherings of the assembly, especially in the Breaking of Bread service. However, a number of scholars have brought into question whether Paul is teaching women's subordination in 1 Corinthians 11:3. The issue as to the exact meaning of the Greek word *kephale* (does it mean 'source' or 'head'?) continues to rumble on.[2] It is also considered that Paul does not insist that every generation of Christian women must wear 'hats' in church.[3]

The issue of women's 'silence' in meetings has also come under scholarly scrutiny. It appears that Paul was calling for silence on the part of women only in certain circumstances, ie, in the judging of prophecy (1 Cor 14:34) and when gathered for whole assembly instruction.[4]

Many churches have, for the past decade or more, made it known that women do not have to wear a head covering and can take part verbally in the Breaking of Bread service. However, in some cases there is still reticence among women to take part in this service. This could be because they are unwilling to risk offending the traditionalists still present. Or, perhaps, the elders of these churches have not ensured that the egalitarianism they teach is followed through in the life of the church. We suggest that equality of men and women be not only consistently taught but also consistently demonstrated. We

---

1. J D Zizioulas, *Being as Communion*, DLT, 1985, 162.
2. See R T France, *Women in the Church's Ministry*, Paternoster Press, 1995, et al.
3. See 1 Cor 11:6 and M Evans, *Christian Brethren Review*, Dec 1982, 33–40.
4. 1 Tim 2:11. See also R T France, op cit, 51ff; S Motyer, *Vox Evangelica*, 1994, 91–102.

recommend that the language we use be examined to see if it is 'inclusive' enough. We also suggest that women be invited to take a more active part in the Breaking of Bread service. This might entail a woman being invited to administer the elements, lead in prayer, or offer a devotional thought from scripture. In the end, the elders need to ensure that what they teach (latently) is what is enacted (manifestly).

The role of children and young people

The South African author, Eddie Prest, writes that 'lip service with regard to the value and importance of children in the church is not matched by actual practice'.[1] At the present time, not all 'Brethren' congregations have a defined policy concerning children taking part in the Breaking of Bread service. They are not alone in this. Writing from an Anglican perspective, Murrie and Pearce point out that children were included in the Lord's Supper in the early church, but add: 'The history of children and communion in the West in later years could be described as a story of children losing their place at the central table of the community.'[2]

The 'Open Brethren' have tended not to include small children in the Breaking of Bread service. However, there is no real reason for this. Traditionally, the 'Brethren' have seen conversion rather than baptism as the point of initiation into the life of the church. Therefore, if parents are confident of their child's personal faith, their exclusion from the Lord's Supper would seem arbitrary. To include the children sends the message that they are important to the church. If children are not included, then the church is not truly gathering as the 'family of God'.

We would suggest that churches consider including the Breaking of Bread as part of the main Sunday morning service. In this way families can attend together, and children can either observe or, with their parents' consent, take part in this central ritual. Diane Murrie puts it well when she writes: 'We journey as a pilgrim church together . . . responsibility for children is the responsibility of the whole church, whether we are related to them or not' (op cit, 17).

---

1. E Prest, *God, Children and the Church*, TFL, Capetown, 1992, 11.
2. D Murrie and S Pearce, *Children and Holy Communion*, Church House Publishing, London, 1997, 3.

Young people

Dieter Zander writes of young people (aged 13–20): 'Perhaps no generation has needed the church so much and sought it so little'.[1] We have noted from empirical research that young people tend to feel excluded from the Breaking of Bread service. This can be attributed to a number of causes, but the chief of these would seem to be the perceived irrelevance of the service. The style, language and music do not seem to 'touch' the younger 'Millenialist' generation.[2]

Here we suggest that churches begin to consider whether there is not a need for a separate youth 'Breaking of Bread', where drama, dance and contemporary music can all be used to facilitate involvement and worship.[3] Or, perhaps, there is a need to review the main Breaking of Bread service so that it might become more 'user-friendly' for younger people. This will take great forethought and planning if it is to meet the needs of the various age groups represented. There is not much point to a service where style and language exclude a significant number of the congregation. To aid their involvement, younger people could be invited to take part, writing down their contributions in advance. The contributions of younger Christians might well help to counteract the cerebralism that has dogged the movement.

Non-Christians at the Breaking of Bread

The 'Brethren' have traditionally guarded the communion table, insisting that non-Christians should not take part. Paul, however, appears to expect non- believers to be present at the Lord's Supper. In the context of the problem of 'eating or drinking' unworthily (1 Cor 11:27–30) he seems to be more concerned with Christians' relationships with each other, rather than non-Christians eating the bread and drinking the wine. Also, Paul speaks in the context of the Lord's Supper in terms of 'proclaiming the Lord's death' (1 Cor 11:26) using a word *(katangello)* that was frequently used in the New testament for preaching the gospel.

We suggest that churches begin to see the Breaking of Bread as an opportunity to witness to the outside world. The 'drama' of the

---

1. D Zander, *Leadership*, Spring 1995, 37.
2. W M Zoba, *Christianity Today*, 1997, 18.
3. Zoba, op cit, 24–25; D Baldwin, *Church Music Quarterly*, April 1997, 20.

bread and wine could speak forcefully to this 'non-book culture'. Members of a 'post-modern' society have no longer a 'meta-narrative' to make sense of life; they are trapped in individualism. This individualism has led some to search again for community and a sense of belonging. The Breaking of Bread can be a place where the church expresses both the forgiveness available in Christ and the opportunity to be a part of a community where egalitarianism is the rule. This could be very attractive to a troubled and lonely unbeliever.

Homes, food and hospitality

We have recognised that, in Corinth, the Lord's Supper was enjoyed in the context of a community meal. We can hardly overestimate the importance of food in much, if not all, of our socialisation. Stephen Happel notes that: 'Food narrates the collective imagination of those who participate in its rituals of gathering, preparation, eating and drinking, and garbage disposal. It involves a set of images, dreams, tastes, choices and values.'[1] Food has always been central to our relating to God.'[2] Happel again: 'Eating and drinking have been the central ritual after initiation. And although these meal rituals have taken many different styles, they nonetheless have focused the weekly Christian assemblies upon food.' (op cit, 4)

Eating together is part of what the Lord's Supper is all about. This concept needs to be explored by churches. It may be that regular 'love feasts' (Jude 12), community meals where the Lord's Supper is included, might become part of congregational life.[3] Home groups might wish to have a meal together and celebrate the Lord's Supper. This would provide for more intimate fellowship and an opportunity to engage in open worship in a non-threatening atmosphere. Whatever the eventual expression of it, we would encourage the churches to explore the concept of taking the Lord's Supper in the context of a meal.

Finally under this heading, we would simply note again that the early churches appeared to meet in homes and this was the likely context in which the Lord's Supper was celebrated.[4] We suggest that

---

1. *The Way*, Jan 1997:3.
2. M Barker, *The Way*, Jan 1997, 17.
3. P Towner, *Evangelical Dictionary of Biblical Theology*, Paternoster, 1996, 495–496.
4. See I H Marshall, *Last Supper and Lord's Supper*, Paternoster, 1980, 108–109.

churches make as much use as possible of members' homes for celebrating the Lord's Supper. For this would provide, not only the opportunity for Christian fellowship at an intimate level, but also the chance to witness by way of Christian hospitality. We know that the modern trend is not to eat together as a family. The church can help families meet together as they eat together.

SACRAMENTS, SIGNS AND SYMBOLS

Traditionally, the 'Brethren' have been Zwinglian in their approach to the elements. For Zwingli, the purpose of the Lord's Supper was to stir up our memory of Christ so that we might feed on him spiritually through faith according to the teaching of Christ recorded in John 6. Through this feeding on him, we will also be united to one another as Paul teaches in 1 Corinthians 10:17. In William Barclay's words, 'for Zwingli the sacrament creates union with each other, and renews union with Christ, and it does both by bringing to our remembrance, through the signs of bread and wine, the death and sacrifice of Christ'.[1]

However, if we limit our understanding of the Lord's Supper to Zwinglian 'memorialism', we are left only remembering Christ rather than encountering him through taking the elements. We are in danger of being left with what Grudem calls, 'a doctrine of the real absence'.[2] We would, therefore, like to suggest that consideration be given to an alternative approach to the Breaking of Bread. This is what is called 'receptionism'. It has helpfully been defined by the Anglican scholar, Roger Beckwith, as the belief that, 'Christ is truly received, though without any change (except in use) in the elements'.[3] That is to say, while the bread and wine remain simply bread and wine, they become the media through which Christ gives himself to us and we receive him through faith.

Examples of this kind of approach can be found in Calvin, and some 'Brethren' writers have also suggested as much. May we propose that congregations be encouraged to heighten their expectation when approaching the Breaking of Bread? Time and teaching

---

1. W Barclay, *The Lord's Supper*, SCM, 1967, 78.
2. W Grudem, *Systematic Theology*, IVP, 1994, 995.
3. *New Dictionary of Theology*, IVP, 1988, 237.

might be given to exploring the concept that, by the Holy Spirit, Christ meets with individuals in a dynamic way as they eat the bread and wine. We recognise that there is nothing magical about the bread and wine, but we surely believe that something deeply spiritual takes place as believers take the elements.[1] R P Martin comes close to the truth when he writes: ' "In remembrance of me" is no bare historical reflection upon the Cross, but a recalling of the crucified and living Christ in such a way that he is personally present in all the fullness of his saving power, and is appropriated by the believer's faith.'[2]

Also, as we live in a world 'of signs and signs about signs', we suggest that church leaders be encouraged to investigate the use of signs and symbols in their churches' life.[3] Symbols can speak of our relationship to God and our relationship to each other. We would therefore particularly recommend the use of the symbol of the cross.[4] A plain wooden cross might be placed at a strategic spot in the place where the church gathers for worship. This is not part of the traditional 'Brethren' approach to worship. However, it might well help members of the congregation to focus on Christ during the Breaking of Bread service.

We would also recommend that congregations make use of what has been called 'liturgical space'.[5] Re-arranging the seating, or even changing the building, would make it possible for the congregation to walk forward to receive communion on some occasions, rather than remaining in their seats, if this were felt to be helpful.[6]

CONCLUSION

We have tried to demonstrate that the 'Brethren' can have every confidence in the biblical basis for their approach to the Breaking of Bread. In the early church there does appear to have been a weekly

---

1. See E P Clowney, *The Church*, IVP, 1995, 74.
2. *Worship in the Early Church*, Eerdmans, 1981, 27.
3. See A M Allchin, *Church Times*, 3 May 1997, 18.
4. See J R W Stott, op cit, 19–25; D A Carson, *The Cross and Christian Ministry*, Baker, 1993, 2–13.
5. G Howes, *Church Building*, March 1997, 54–55.
6. See R Giles, *Re-pitching the Tent*, Canterbury Press, Norwich, 9; M Marshall, *Free to Worship*, Marshall Pickering, 1992, 181.

(if not more often!) gathering of Christians for both a social meal and a time focusing on Christ which included the use of spiritual gifts. There is, however, a need for some radical re-thinking.

This meal and worship time seems to fit best in the context of a home meeting. Perhaps our principal difficulty in making the most of these gatherings is that we have tried to force into the larger, more impersonal church context an activity that should, instead, take place in the more intimate setting of a family home. We suggest that church leaders and congregations give a great deal of thought to having this 'meal with meaning' regularly in members' homes. This does not preclude the gathering of the whole church for a corporate meal and worship. In an age of crippling individualism and desperate isolation, this meal could be used by God to build Christian community and proclaim Jesus to a world that still desperately needs what he has to offer.

5

Music, movement and silence in worship

John Allan

John Allan is senior youth worker at Belmont Chapel, Exeter. He has written and lectured extensively on subjects such as youth culture, cults and the occult.

THE SILENCE OF THE BIBLE

One of the annoying things about the scriptures is that often they don't tell us all we would like to know. On some subjects, there is tantalisingly little written for our instruction, and we might wonder why God has allowed this to happen; you or I would not have managed things thus. We would have inserted a couple of verses unambiguously clarifying the doctrine of the Trinity, and so have undermined a whole century of Jehovah's Witness confusion. We would have written long, detailed directions for the participation of women in church services and the precise mode of baptism to be used, and so have avoided thousands of hours of theological controversy and bitterness. And – I suspect – we would have said a little more about worship.

Worship is never defined or described in detail in either the New Testament or the Old. Hence Christians have problems in deciding what we are actually commanded to do. What are the limits of our freedom? Are some activities acceptable, and others not? Are we to follow slavishly an approved liturgy composed by other men? Or are we to make a determined drive for simplicity, spontaneity and originality – at the possible cost of depth, beauty and theological richness? And what physical or mental activities are involved anyway? Must we restrict ourselves to the style of the early church – in which case, out goes the organ – or are we free to open ourselves up

79

to a bewildering range of innovative techniques of which the apostles never dreamed?

How different it all is from those religions which place tremendous stress upon their ceremonies. In some sacred books there are detailed, pedantic instructions for every stage of a ritual or sacrifice or sacrament. Roman augurs followed a strict code of rules in trying to read the omens; and if one minor detail went wrong, even at an advanced stage of the proceedings, the whole procedure had to be scrapped and started again. This is the way that magic works, and still does in our own day (as the books of people like Dion Fortune and Gareth Knight demonstrate). Divine power depends on getting the ceremony right. Otherwise, it doesn't work.

But the Bible's reticence about worship methods is precisely what we might expect from the Bible's view of God. For he is a personal, sovereign being, not an impersonal natural force which can be manipulated by initiates. Peter Berger has written a suggestive essay in which he contrasts the pagan nature religions of the Canaanites with the true worship of God for which the prophets contended. He points out that the seductive appeal of Canaanite religion was that it did not involve any personal dealings, any 'I – Thou' encounter, with a God who was loving, jealous and demanding:

> The human being's fundamental religious quest is to establish contact with divine forces and beings that transcend him. The cult of sacred sexuality provided this contact in a way that was both easy and pleasurable. The gods were as close as one's own genitalia; to establish contact with them, when all was said mythologically and all was done ritually, one only had to do what, after all, one wanted to do anyway . . .
>
> The sacred sexuality complex was repudiated by those who spoke for Yahweh because it violated their central understanding of both God and humanity . . . Israel encountered its God as a God of history, through the mighty acts that were the foundation of the covenant . . .
>
> Unlike the cult of sacred sexuality, the cult of Yahweh did not lead to otherworldly ecstasy; rather, it directed people back into the world, where their task was to do God's will in human affairs. Worship here was inevitably linked with the whole gamut of moral concerns in society – with social justice, with the right

relations between nations and classes, with the protection of the weak.[1]

Biblical worship is a two-way process: God gives to us and we give to God. Two independent personalities encounter one another. Paul insists in Acts 17:25 that our God 'is not served with human hands, as if he needed anything', and the word used here for 'serve' is *therapeuo*, a word never used of Christian worship. Yet it describes some forms of non-Christian worship perfectly. The basic meaning of the word is 'to take care of' (it is the word from which we derive such words as 'therapy' and 'therapeutic'). This is precisely what the Hare Krishna follower does in his life in the temple. Every morning, the temple gods have to be taken reverently out of their 'beds' and put on their shelf in the temple. Food has to be offered to them. They have to be washed. At night, they are put back in bed again. And throughout the day, the devotee spends a large part of his time quite literally taking care of the gods. This is one form of worship.

But such one-way worship is profoundly non-Christian. The worship of the God of Israel involves an interplay of what God supplies and what we contribute. God does not want the mechanical obedience of robots, following a prescribed pattern of unvarying service in an unthinking way. He wants to draw out of us something which is individual, creative, our own.

This is why the psalms speak so often of 'a new song'. The creative edge in worship, not just the tired reciting of acceptable forms, is vitally important. And it is why Revelation tells us that 'the glory and honour of the nations' will be brought into the heavenly city (Rev 21:26). Even in the direct presence of God, when worship reaches its eternal climax, human creative achievement can and must be blended into the great paean of praise.

HUMAN FREEDOM IN WORSHIPPING METHODS

So much has been taught down through the years, in 'Brethren' circles, about the divine pattern for the construction of the tabernacle

---

1. P Berger, 'Cakes for the Queen of Heaven', in *Facing up to Modernity*, Penguin, 1977, 243, 245–246.

and the feasts of Jehovah, that we sometimes fail to notice the element of human freedom which God built in, right from the start, to the worship he had commanded. We must not focus so exclusively upon God's part in designing Old Testament worship that we ignore Israel's contribution. For one thing, although the materials used in the construction of the tabernacle are listed in detail, Exodus 25 makes it clear that these materials came together in an offering 'from each man whose heart prompts him to give'. In other words, God organized the materials once they were provided, but each of the human beings involved had the freedom to decide upon the part that he personally wanted to play. There is more freedom when men of skill are appointed (Exod 31) 'to engage in all kinds of craftsmanship': they have to produce the sacred objects exactly as God has directed, but room is left for their personal creativity, 'to make artistic designs for work in gold, silver and bronze'.

Most notably, although the furnishings of the tabernacle and the sacrifices to be offered are closely prescribed, the same is not true of the manner of worship. Did they sing? Did they dance? We know little of the style of those days, and the scriptures are no help to us. God left room for methods of worship to develop as culturally and historically appropriate.

When, later in history, the temple worship was established, we gain no sense from the scriptures that this was a bad thing – even though it involved changes in the strict pentateuchal pattern of worship; even though it was David's personal idea, rather than a sudden command from God. And, centuries later, the synagogue emerged spontaneously, changing the style of worship yet again, although God had given no new direction that this was to happen. Jesus used the synagogues as places of worship (and, for that matter, Herod's temple); and early Christian congregations patterned their worship and government on synagogue practices. There was obviously nothing wrong with the synagogue just because it was a human invention.

Perhaps, sometimes, we who are 'Brethren' have been overly concerned with strict purity of practice. 'See that thou do all things according to the pattern shown thee in the mount' is a text which has often haunted our worship style. In the Darby-inspired quest for a totally, biblically pure fellowship, we have tried to find rules and patterns where the scripture actually leaves us free. (I grew up in an assembly, for instance, where the 'by-laws' included the idea that brethren and sisters should sit at opposite sides of the hall; that the bread should be passed literally from hand to hand, since putting it on a plate would be 'a symbol of Egypt'; and so on. Other assemblies have had laws about not permitting 'ministry' before the bread was broken, not permitting different brethren to give thanks individually for loaf and cup, never breaking the bread before a certain amount of time had elapsed in the service.)

MUSIC, MOVEMENT, SILENCE, AND WORSHIP

What has all this to do with the professed subject of this essay? Simply this: that music, movement and silence are all possible methods of worship, and if we want to determine their usefulness to us in worshipping God, scripture will not help us much directly. Scripture does not legislate about our methods; space is left for human freedom; the way to assess our methods is not to ask, 'But did they really do this in biblical times?' – but instead, 'Do these methods really help us achieve the purposes of worship?'

It is important to stress this point, since so many of the current crop of evangelical paperbacks arguing for or against the use of dance, drama, rock music and the arts in worship try to prove their case by listing all the places in the Bible where such activities are mentioned. The result is stalemate, because advocates of dance can point to a few verses that mention their speciality, and their opponents can point to thousands that don't; supporters of rock music can quote texts which refer to loud and rhythmical noises, and their opponents can point out that this is all Old Testament, and a ram's horn trumpet can't be compared to a Vox AC 30 anyway. The only clear conclusion from the biblical evidence – although it is a conclusion both sides seem to resist – is that the scriptures are supremely uninterested in the pros and cons of specific methods. The real question is what they achieve.

What are the purposes of worship? That is dealt with elsewhere in this volume. Here it will be enough to note that the key New Testament words for worship (*proskyneō, leitourgeō, latreuō*) combine three basic ideas: *affection*, intelligent *recognition of the authority* of the person worshipped, and *submission to serve*. In other words, the total response of the human personality to God: emotions, mind and will. Worship thus has three purposes: *release* of the emotions; *recognition* with the mind; and *resolve* of the will in gearing itself for fresh acts of service.

It is not difficult to think of historical cases of the distinguished use of music, movement and silence in worship. Music has been with the Christian church from the start, going right back to the early days when a perplexed Roman governor wrote to his emperor, 'They sing a hymn to Christ as a god.' Different kinds of movement have been important in worship in various cultures – from the ritual movements and symbolic actions of Catholic and Orthodox traditions, to the uninhibited self-expression through dance of some black denominations and Latin American Pentecostals. Silence was an important tool in the mystical tradition – Thomas A Kempis, for one, says a lot about it – as well as among Quakers and Quietists.

But do these methods – music, movement and silence – genuinely achieve the purposes of worship? And if so, in what forms? For there are serious questions which need to be asked. Isn't it possible that a wrong application of methods can introduce us to experiences which we fondly imagine to be worship – but which are actually something quite different?

Music today raises the problem of contemporary rock. Is it a fitting style for the worship of God, or is it 'devil music', full of dangerous jungle rhythms? Aren't all these new choruses lamentably superficial, repulsively sickly, and sometimes downright misleading? While some are finding new avenues of worship through movement, and writing books with titles like *Praise Him in the Dance* and *Moving Prayer*, others are writing equally trenchantly that 'the dance has more potential for evil than anything else we do in Christian circles today'.[1]

But surely no one could object to silence? Well, perhaps. Ralph Martin points out that in the Old Testament 'praise involves the use of words audibly expressed. Silent prayer is not a Hebrew practice',[2] and he cites Eli, who thought Hannah was drunk because her lips were moving but she was making no sound. 'I do not believe it is necessarily true that we are worshipping God when we make a lot of racket', wrote A W Tozer. 'But not infrequently worship is audible.'[3]

The few verses in the Bible which seem to speak about silence in

---

1. B Edwards, *Shall we dance?*, Evangelical Press, 1984, 98.
2. R P Martin, *The Worship of God*, Eerdmans, 1982, 20.
3. A W Tozer, *Whatever happened to Worship?*, STL/Kingsway, 1986, 16.

worship (such as Hab 2:20) are actually not about worship at all, but set against the background of a law court – in which the guilty party remains silent because he has no defence to offer. (The same is true of that curious half hour of silence in Rev 8:1 – silence speaks of judgment, not worship.) In the New Testament epistles, silence is mentioned only as a restriction upon participation in worship, not a means of worship in itself.

Taking all of this together, it would be possible to argue that the normative biblical picture of worship is of people being compelled to speak – of impulses of devotion that demand verbal expression, otherwise 'the stones would immediately cry out' – and that an unscriptural emphasis upon silence will lead into an introverted, idiosyncratic mysticism which separates worshipper from worshipper and ends in the fanciful pursuit of an 'inner light' which is no more than a subjective fantasy.

And so the questions mount up. How do we tackle them? Here I want to do it by asking two questions. First: do these three possible worship methods actually achieve each of the purposes of worship – release, recognition and resolve? And, second: if they do, how should they be employed for maximum benefit? What is the distinctive contribution that each of the three can make?

RECOGNITION, RELEASE, RESOLVE

First, then, let us ask some questions about the purposes of worship. Do these three methods help us to achieve a recognition of God's greatness? Do they affect our mental appreciation in worship?

Music obviously does. Teaching can often be much more effective when set to an insistent rhythm ('Thirty days hath September'; 'i before e except after c'). Jesus knew this secret, and scholars, such as Joachim Jeremias, have shown that distinct Aramaic rhythms lay behind the teaching Jesus passed on to his disciples. In the Old Testament, several of the psalms clearly served an educational function: recitations of the history of God's mighty acts, such as Psalm 136, taught the young and reminded the old, all in the context of worship.

In the New Testament text, there are several embedded passages (Eph 5:14; 1 Tim 3:16; Phil 2: 6–11; 2 Tim 2:11–14; Jas 1:17) where it seems the writer has quoted a section from a current Christian hymn.

Obviously, hymns were useful in helping people remember the key facts of the faith – and could sum them up better than the writer felt he could himself.

How does movement affect our recognition? First, participation in symbolic actions can make theoretical ideas more concrete, provoke moments of awareness and insight; this is the result of the symbolic act at the very heart of our worship:

> Here, O my Lord, I see thee face to face;
> Here faith can touch and handle things unseen.

'No Gospel like this feast', we sing. For the physical action of taking bread and wine and passing it from hand to hand *makes actual* what would otherwise be merely an academic concept. Other kinds of movement and action might then have a similar, if less central, effect in bringing home to our recognition some of the central truths of our relationship to God and one another.

But, second, movement in which we may not be involved personally, but merely watch as spectators (a performance of dance, for example), can also provoke recognition in a unique way. I have seen Springs Dance Company evoke the wonder of the resurrection unforgettably in a worship service, in a way that could not have been equalled verbally. Brian Edwards' critical book *Shall We Dance?* complains that dance and drama are inferior to the spoken word because they 'have generally to be interpreted'[1] This, it seems to me, is exactly wrong. Dance and drama can speak more immediately and powerfully, can provoke a more direct crisis of recognition, than words can manage.

What of silence? It has been a remarkable feature of history that churches with a worship style involving plenty of reflective silence (such as the 'Brethren' and the Society of Friends) have typically produced thoughtful, careful people with a more stringent intellectual approach to faith than those reared in churches whose worship majors on noise and excitement, or predictable liturgy. Silence allows time for a whirlwind sequence of conflicting impressions to be analysed into its elements and sifted thoroughly.

So much for recognition. But there is also release. Here, again, all three methods have a contribution to make. Music, obviously – the

---

1. Edwards, op cit, 88–89.

emotional release of belting out 'Bold I approach the eternal throne . . .' is something we have all experienced. And movement – for watching a well-executed piece of dance, drama or mime can stir the emotions unforgettably. I can still remember examples I witnessed ten or fifteen years ago, although all other details of the service in which they featured have faded completely from my mind.

It is not natural for us to sit still at times of deep emotional experience. 'Let Israel rejoice in their Maker', urges Psalm 149, '. . . let them praise his name with dancing'. Rosemary Budd argues: 'Our physical energies are a major element in our lives whether we recognize them or not . . . If we recognize our energies, we can harness them for great good.'[1] Movement in worship can release emotions powerfully and effectively, because 'body language' affects our state of mind. It is no coincidence that emotion is often hard to detect in meetings where the ground rules dictate two permissible position – standing to sing and sitting for all else – with no variation contemplated.

And silence? Everyone who has ever been in love has known moments when words are inadequate and unnecessary: the wondering silence of two young lovers staring into one another's eyes, the companionable, trusting silence of a long-married couple who can almost communicate telepathically. Sometimes, worship will touch these emotional heights. And a period of silence can deepen what would otherwise be a passing moment's impulse.

It has been suggested that speaking in tongues is really a regression to the pre-speech phase of infancy – when we make sounds, but they have no logical referent; we express ourselves with total freedom, unconstrained by the demands of grammar and vocabulary. To speak in tongues releases us to express what we could not otherwise; some emotions in worship defy confinement to normal vocabulary. Perhaps (especially for non-tongues speakers) silence can serve the same function.

Do music, movement and silence also help us with the resolve aim of worship? Music, it is easy to see, can be powerful in reinforcing decisions we need to make – as anyone can tell you who has been brought into the kingdom during the singing of 'Just as I am'. Recently, after I had spoken to a group of young people on a houseparty, a young musician present quietly played a song he had

---

1. R Budd, *Moving Prayer; an introduction to a deeper devotional life*, MARC, 1987, 42.

written himself, 'To be more like Jesus'. The atmosphere of worship as he finished was almost overpowering.

Music has often been useful in strengthening resolve in moments of crisis. Just before he, and a group of his colleagues, went out into a dangerous, costly mission, Geoffrey Bull records, one of them suddenly began to sing, 'King of my life I crown Thee now'. It was an unforgettable moment, and just what the group needed. Was there even an element of the same thing on the evening on which, Matthew tells us, 'when they had sung a hymn, they went out to the Mount of Olives'?

Drama or dance can have the same impact in focusing decision. For our first evangelistic presentation at the Greenbelt Festival, some years ago, the committee decided that, after the preacher had finished, no music or spoken words would follow. Instead, Geoffrey Stevenson would end with a silent mime challenging non-Christians to commitment – and the audience would leave with that unspoken appeal as their final memory. Over thirty people accepted Christ that evening.

Other kinds of symbolic movement – standing up, walking to the front, raising a hand – are often used in evangelism to signal commitment and offer a concrete chance to make up one's mind. Creatively used, movement can serve that kind of function in worship too.

After years of 'Just as I am', Billy Graham began to find that silence could be just as effective as music in bringing people to personal crises of decision. Sometimes the breathless hush as people from all over the auditorium left their seats and filtered to the front could be even more compelling than a hymn. As in evangelism, so in worship. Leaving a space for people to make their own promises to God can be an effective thing to do. Often the stillness for several minutes at the end of an affecting worship service is an indication that people are having private dealings with God, all over the room. The worst thing to do at such a point would be to give out another chorus.

Used in the right way, then, music, movement and silence can all fulfil the three basic purposes of worship. Which leads to our second question. What is the right way? What limits do we set to the use of music, movement and silence in worship?

THE ROLE OF MUSIC

Music crops up often in scripture. The Old Testament mentions all sorts of instruments, both loud and soft, both percussive and otherwise. 'It can be assumed', historians tell us, 'that . . . the singing of the Psalms was always accompanied by musical instruments.'[1]

There were probably no musical instruments in use in the early church, but experimentation and creativity were encouraged. Tertullian tells us that all members were free to participate by words of scripture or 'songs of their own invention'. Ralph Martin believes that the 'spiritual songs' of Colossians 3:16 and Ephesians 5:19 were 'the result of immediate inspiration, as in the scene in 1 Corinthians 14:26 where improvised compositions. . . are brought to the assembly and used in worship. They may well have been no more than single-line statements.'[2]

Scholars have often debated the difference between 'psalms', 'hymns' and 'spiritual songs'. Most would agree that it is impossible to define these terms clearly. But it is certain that Paul uses them to indicate an enormously wide range of musical activity: employing the text of scripture, individual compositions, spur-of-the-moment improvisations, credal statements in musical form, personal songs of devotion.

Not all Christians have agreed that such an abundance of musical variation should be possible in the church. (Zwingli, for instance, wanted to abolish all congregational singing; Calvin was ill at ease with anything more than metrical psalms.) And, in our own day, we have witnessed the rise of a new, ersatz pop art form: rock music. Increasingly, now, the rhythms of rock are invading worship music, and the instruments associated with it – drums, bass guitars, synthesisers – are appearing in church services. Is this a phenomenon which should worry us?

John Blanchard's book, *Pop Goes the Gospel*, has no doubts. 'When the beat overrides the other elements in a song the communication level is significantly changed to one which is primarily physical and often specifically sexual . . . the element of relentless beat in rock music increases the danger of a shallow, emotional, unthinking response.' He quotes approvingly David Wilkerson's comment that

1. K H Bartels, in *The New International Dictionary of New Testament Theology*, Vol 3, Paternoster, 1978, article 'Song'.
2. Martin, op cit, 53.

'I also have a sense, an inner knowledge, that the gentle Holy Spirit is not comfortable in the atmosphere this music creates.'[1]

It is hard to argue with comments like this. Blanchard is appealing to a psychological analysis of rock's effect which few psychologists would subscribe to, and at best is unproven; Wilkerson is arguing from inner intuition – and that is inaccessible to reasoned argument. There are really no musical, moral or psychological grounds for damning any particular musical form as 'inappropriate for Christians'. As Larry Norman pointed out, 'The sonic structure of music is basically neutral'.[2] In the Middle Ages, the interval of the augmented fourth was banned from church music, because it belonged to the Devil. But no-one bothers about using it today.

Arguments from the dissolute lifestyle, or occult interests, of certain rock stars are beside the point. The medium has been misused, but it has become the major form of cultural expression in music for the greater part of the British population this century. Its misuse by some people should not prevent us from employing it to create an authentically modern, genuine response in worship to God. Says Andrew Maries, musical director of St Michael le Belfry:

> To begin to make moral judgements as to the worth of different styles of music and the moral calibre of composers and performers really does become a nonsense. So many of the great classical composers could hardly be considered committed Christians, and yet they produced masterpieces which reveal something of the meaning and glory of life. Their works are windows on eternity through which we may well witness God.[3]

And yet – however much scripture encourages the *new song* – lively appreciation of past tradition always marks biblical worship, too. The psalms were not abandoned in the early church. The antiphonal choir complexities of post-exilic worship were a new thing in Israel, but the music reflected the old songs of past centuries. There are dangers in a headlong rush into modernity; throwing out

---

1. J Blanchard, *Pop goes the Gospel*, Evangelical Press, 1983. 17, 133. Odd to find a non-charismatic Calvinist like Blanchard – who criticises advocates of rock music for their woolly subjectivism – using evidence of this kind.
2. From the sleeve notes of his *Solid Rock* albums.
3. A Maries, *One Heart, one Voice: the rich and varied resource of music in worship*, Hodder, 1986, 98.

Hymns of Faith when we acquire *Songs of Fellowship* may turn out to be a premature move.

For one thing, the modern style of music encourages emotional expression and depth; that is its strength. It does not encourage intricate expression of truth, and it is vulnerable to mawkish sentimentality; that is its weakness. We need the strong hymns of previous ages too.

Also, rock music in society is often associated with showmanship, shallow excitement, and self-promotion. If it is to be recovered for use in worship, it needs to be divorced from these tendencies. We have learned a great deal about how to do that in the last ten years. And blending the new with the old is the most effective way of reaping the benefits of the contemporary style, without losing the perspective of all we have learned about worshipping God from the past.

What can music do that other worship media can't? Music is a tremendously *communal* activity; it brings the church together as little else can. 'The first Christians thought of "hymns" as a means of mutual encouragement and challenge aimed horizontally at a group of fellow believers.'[1] And music provides a means of expression for the less articulate. It is no coincidence that most movements of the Holy Spirit among the oppressed and downtrodden have produced great music – from Negro spirituals to nineteenth-century Salvation Army creativity to the harmonies of unschooled Welsh miners. No method is essential to worship. But music would be very difficult to do without.

MOVEMENT: THE CHRISTIAN VIEW OF THE BODY

Early in its history, the Christian church was strongly influenced by Greek philosophy. And in some respects the malign influences of Platonic thought have tended to cling around Christianity ever since. This is especially true of the attitude Christians have often adopted to the human body.

For Plato and his popularisers, the body was basically evil, the loathsome prison of the pure and valuable spirit. Growth in spirituality comes as we de-emphasize the material realm and concentrate on the life of the spirit instead.

---

1. Martin, op cit, 53.

The Hebrew view of the body never made this sharp distinction of the 'spiritual bit' and the 'physical bit' in man. 'Don't you know that your body is the temple of the Holy Spirit. . .?' inquires Paul. 'So use your bodies for God's glory' (1 Cor 6:19–20 GNB). At creation, 'man became a living soul' (Gen 2:7 AV) – the soul is not a detachable possession which man was given along with a body, but inextricably involved with the body as part of the complex reality of being human.

But the Greek distrust for the body eventually started to influence Christian thinkers; and anchorites, flagellants and hermits began to pride themselves on their mistreatment of their bodies. Origen, as a young man, tried to prove his zeal by castrating himself (a deed he later regretted). And the Platonic attitude in less extreme forms has never quite left Christianity alone since, as Macaulay and Barrs[1] have demonstrated.

The Platonic attitude to the body can produce two very different approaches to worship: first, a horror of anything fleshly, and thus a fear of undue movement, physical expressions, dance and drama; second, a struggle to release the spirit from the body. Plato said that this could happen through 'divine madness' and, in Christian circles, this has often led to the attempt to develop 'the things of the Spirit' by abandoning the body to ecstasy. Neither of these responses is Christian.

The Hebrew attitude to the body, however, leads to a recognition of three facts. First, that a body has a place in worship, as a valuable part of creation. Elisabeth Elliot claims:

> More spiritual failure is due, I believe, to this cause than to any other: the failure to recognize this living body as having anything to do with worship or holy sacrifice.[2]

'For far too long', complains Rosemary Budd, 'many of us as Christians have found it terribly difficult to understand ourselves as bodies, a physical expression of personality in a physical universe. We've tried to pray without bodies.'[3]

Second, the Hebrew attitude recognises that the body is not a channel of sacredness – the mistake made by the Canaanite 'sacred sexuality' religions we examined earlier. God communicates primar-

---

1. R Macauley and J Barrs, *Christianity with a human Face*, IVP, 1979.
2. Budd, op cit, 42.
3. Budd, op cit, 42.

ily through rationality, through propositional statements, and while sensitive use of the body's movements in worship can assist our understanding, it cannot become a substitute for rational appreciation of God.

Third, the Hebrew picture demands that we also recognize the fallenness of the body. 'I see another law at work in the members of my body', writes Paul, 'waging war against the law of my mind' (Rom 7:23). The possibility of evil is always there. Which is not a reason for shunning the body's potential in worship – but simply being careful to exploit it watchfully and honestly.

It is true that New Testament worship did not include dancing, as Herbert Carson points out in his book *Hallelujah!* Carson asks why the church eschewed such a powerful means of communication, since it was known and practised in the Roman world. But earlier in his discussion he has supplied his own answer: dance was a practice exclusively related to pagan ecstatic religion; there was not much use of it for other purposes. For the Christians to have incorporated it, at that stage, would have been unthinkable.

But dance and movement played an important part in Old Testament worship. Or did they? In his book *Shall We Dance?*, Brian Edwards has bravely – if perversely – tried to prove that they did not. He claims that most of the words commonly translated 'dance' can mean something else, that when dancing is mentioned it is not as a part of worship (or, as in Judg 21:21, it reflects a decadent form of worship), and that David's famous dancing before the ark in 2 Samuel 6:14 was 'exceptional', 'the spontaneous overflow of an excited worshipper'.[1]

This argument will not do. Dance was a common feature of Oriental festivals, and it would have been strange – strange enough to require comment somewhere – if the nation of Israel had been markedly different from all their neighbours. The Hebrew word for 'festival' comes from the verb *hagag*, to dance. Edwards suggests that David did not exactly dance – ' "Skip for joy" would be more accurate' – but 2 Samuel 6:1–14 is clearly describing a set of deliberate ceremonial procedures, not a momentary burst of unscheduled enthusiasm. Psalms 149:3 and 150:4 both exhort worshippers to 'praise his name with dancing'. Edwards counters that the verses 'do not set out to discuss the content of Jewish worship in the temple;

---

1. Edwards, op cit, 57.

they simply claim that everything in the life of God's people, from dancing to war, should be to the honour of God'.[1] If so, one would expect both psalms to mention a wide range of human social activities which could be unexpected avenues for the praise of God. But they do not. They simply elaborate a list of ceremonial implements of praise – the trumpet, the tambourine, the harp . . . The obvious conclusion, for an unprejudiced reader, is that dancing is just one item in a list of recognised worshipping methods.

The use of physical movement opens up many possibilities for worship: artistic presentations to add a dimension to a service; free participatory spontaneous movement; physical positioning and symbolic gesture. We must guard against mentally reducing the list to a few obvious, well-worn routines. For instance, many house church people who take pride in having rediscovered dance in worship have really gone no further than the curious, stylized, self-conscious little dance step cruelly christened by onlookers 'the charismatic hop'. Freedom has frozen into liturgy. We 'Brethren' know all about that.

Again, we must guard against becoming too pompous about it all. Surely I'm not the only one who finds Rosemary Budd unduly fanciful when she writes that hands held under a Bible 'are a symbol of receptivity to its contents', or unduly programmatic when she advises us practically: 'Your pelvis is very important. Tuck your tail in and check that the lumbar vertebrae are bent neither forwards nor backwards.'[2] It sounds faintly ludicrous. But there again, if the lumbar vertebrae are part of a good God's creation, perhaps they have their own humble part to play in praising him.

SILENCE AND ITS USES

Another result of Platonism, through the ideas of Dionysius the Areopagite, has been the *via negativa*, the 'negative way' of acquiring spiritual knowledge which has characterised Christian mysticism for many centuries.

Spiritual growth, according to Dionysius, does not come through understanding who God is and what his blessings are. Rather we

---

1. Ibid, 61.
2. Budd, op cit, 79, 46.

must remove all positive statements about God until we are left with silence – the bare communion of the soul with God.[1]

St John of the Cross wrote about the experience in these words:

> The man who truly there has come
> Of his own self must shed the guise;
> Of all he knew before the sum
> Seems far beneath that wondrous prize:
> And in this lore he grows so wise
> That he remains, though knowing naught,
> Transcending knowledge with his thought.[2]

Evangelicals disagree about how to assess this kind of spirituality. But all agree that, first, it is the province of a few rare people, rather than a practical possibility for every Christian; second, even if genuine, it comes so close to the experience of mystics in other religions (Sufis, for instance, or the writers of the Upanishads) that it can lead to religious relativism and heresy.

Perhaps the reason that the scriptures pay so little attention to silence is that the silence of mysticism can be a dangerous route to travel. Speech is more characteristic of a religion in which 'it is in the nature of God to speak. The second person of the Holy Trinity is called the *Word*.'[3] Edmund Clowney insists, 'Christian meditation, therefore, looks to Jesus. It treasures his words and remembers his deeds. The vision of God is not a mystical achievement requiring prodigious feats of trance-like concentration.'[4]

And so the scriptures have little time for the kind of silence which blanks out normal thought processes. This does not mean, however, that all silence is necessarily a bad thing. Periods of silence can heighten thought, as well as depressing it; can reinforce ideas, as well as obliterating them. Silence in worship can legitimately achieve three useful objectives at least.

First, it prevents worship becoming a 'spectator sport'. It suddenly removes from the worshipper all outside stimulus, and throws him in upon his own resources; for a short while now he will

---

1. Macauley and Barrs, op cit, 42.
2. 'Verses written after an estasy of high exaltation', in *St John of the Cross: Poems*, tr R Campbell, Penguin Classics, 1968, 47–48.
3. A W Tozer, *The Pursuit of God*, Aslan Paperbacks, 1968, 75.
4. E Clowney, *Christian Meditation*, IVP, 1980, 23.

be unable to coast along as a passive observer of prayers, hymns and readings offered for his benefit by other people. Silence *personalizes* worship.

Second, paradoxically enough, silence draws worshippers closer together. We are never so aware of one another as when a group of people sit together without talking. (For example, watch a carriage full of Underground passengers when the train stops between stations!) A shared, almost palpable silence expresses deep communion more eloquently than the singing of a dozen hymns.

Third, silence can change the direction of worship. In the stillness it is possible for worshippers to listen more closely to the promptings of the Holy Spirit, to hear him saying something unexpected which would otherwise be missed in the noisy forward thrust of an all-action period of worship. As a result, the worship time can have quite a different outcome to what anyone present might initially have expected.

Of course, silence can be misused. There is a fine line between the reverential silence of worshippers awed at the presence of God's holiness, and the bored silence of a bunch of 'Brethren' in one more standard 'morning meeting' with nothing new to say. Silence, like any other method, can be overused and cheapened.

But it is good that it should be so! God has not given us strict and specific instructions about how much of which elements to incorporate at which moments in order to produce an approved worship service. Instead, he has left it up to us. The methods we use are at our discretion. And that is the awful joy, the responsibility, the delight and freedom of worshipping in Spirit and in truth.

Sometimes the silences of scripture are a thoroughly good thing.

6

Intergenerational worship

Eddie Prest[1]

After 31 years on the staff of Scripture Union in South Africa, 16 of them as general director, Eddie has been acting in a leadership training and consultative capacity for the past 11 years. He serves numerous denominations, including the Presbyterian Church of South Africa, and is the author of four books.

INTRODUCTION

Though the word may be inelegant, the concept of intergenerational worship (IGW) is both biblical and relevant to the practice of worship in the modern world. Before exploring it, we will attempt to define it.

A *generation* comes into existence when an age-group identifies itself as being different from other age-groups, develops a sense of exclusive identity, and resists suggestions of interacting with other generation or age-groups. Living, as we do, at a time when age-grouping is important, it is not surprising that generationalism has become deeply entrenched and accepted as the norm for any organisation. One church leader has lamented the fact that his church comprised no less than five different groups, each identified by age, each with its own agenda, and each fiercely pursuing its own agenda.

Intergenerationalism is a concept and process in church life which is designed to relate generations in common fellowship and learning experiences. It affirms that people of different ages can come together in meaningful fellowship and enjoy common worship and

---

1. This chapter is based on one of the author's books, *From One Generation to Another*, with permission. Eddie may be contacted at TFL Publishing, PO Box 38721, Pinelands, 7404, Cape Town, South Africa.

learning experiences to the significant benefit of all. While accepting the uniqueness and value of each generation, it attempts to find common denominators which facilitate a generational overflow.

This is no new idea. More than a century ago, C H Spurgeon said:

> I feel more and more that it is a mistake to divide children from the congregation. I believe in special services for children, but I would also have them worship with us. I like to see the congregation made up, not of all young, not all old, but some of all sorts gathered together.

Nor is it an exclusively Christian idea. Margaret Mead, the well known anthropologist, who is also also a grandmother, writes: 'Children are like a renewing force . . . when a community stops taking notice of its children, then something goes radically wrong with the whole community.'

Yet traditional worship remains exclusively adult, and the idea of people of all ages worshipping together is regarded as unrealistic if not fanciful. Most recognise that children need adults in order to worship God, but the idea that adults need children to normalise them is rarely acknowledged.

BIBLICAL FOUNDATIONS

Scripture reveals the importance of modifying the extreme individualism so characteristic of western philosophy by a strong sense of corporate identity which not only holds the past, present and future together, but also embraces clans, families and individuals – including children – in a single whole. In biblical times, children, representing the new generation, were not merely included in the religion of Israel; they were deeply incorporated into it. Four things should be noted.

- *The theological importance of children gave them a place of value and importance to God's people.*

They were God's gift, and he remained their ultimate possessor. Therefore they belonged not only to their parents but also to God's people.

98

- *The belief that they were able to experience, worship and praise God afforded them an important place in the religious life of Israel.*

Children participated meaningfully in the Sabbath celebrations, and the joy of thanksgiving at the festivals of Israel. For example, at the celebration of the Passover, three or four generations would have participated, stretching across the total age-range. Involvement would have taken place at all levels, from the youngest boy asking the trigger question to doting elders delighting in the participation of the third and fourth generation.

- *The importance of children as the 'future of Israel' forged a close and bonding relationship between old and young.*

Children were regarded as the bearers of Israel's name, faith and values into the future (for a couple, childlessness spelled no future for the family). As in a relay race, children would receive the baton of faith, run with it into the future, and hand it on to their children.

- *The corporate nature of childhood called for a caring environment in which their sense of belonging was strong.*

Since human nature, created in the image of the triune God, is corporate, a family environment is essential. This is secured by an extended range of generations in which children receive the strong social and spiritual support of other members of the 'family' in order to grow up in what God has ordained for them – a complete people.

A Conducive Environment for Intergenerational Worship

If a church is to be able to create an atmosphere conducive to the practice of intergenerational worship, adults must realise and appreciate four things.

- *Children are 'people too', and can be addressed as such, provided the words and concepts used are understood and relevant.*

From a very young age, children possess developed ideas and feelings and a real ability to work through problems and reach conclusions. If addressed in a dignified manner, children can be expected to respond in kind. Often, however, because children are so much smaller physically, it is difficult for adults to connect conceptually with them on an eye-to-eye level, and so they are addressed in an infantile manner and react appropriately – 'like children'. But when adults overcome this obstacle an environment develops that is highly conducive to an intergenerational experience.

- *Children have a developed capacity for understanding and experiencing God, and for asking profound theological questions.*

Dr Sophia Cavaletti wrote a book entitled, *The Religious Potential of the Child*, based on thirty years experience of working with children. In it, she wrote of three-to-six year old children: 'All children experience God . . . have as humans an essential or natural religious inclination. This innate capacity must be stimulated and nurtured if children are to develop fully.'

- *Children are capable of ministering to adults in a very special way, given the opportunity.*

Before the opportunity can be given, the adult may need to undergo a transforming experience similar to becoming a child again! (Andre Malraux has said that, 'When there is no childness left in man . . . the only thing he is good for is to die.') Elizabeth Baer, writing in *The Friends Journal*, forcefully makes the point that adults can be ministered to by children:

> I'm discovering that my spiritual renewal is promoted by children – not only my children, but all the children at the meeting . . . For me children speak in vivid ways that I am too limited to admit, much less express. Their honesty, spontaneity and heartfelt response teach us a great deal. I am learning from these little people, who may in some ways be spiritual giants compared to adults who try to be 'of God'.

- *Christian education is related far less to words than to presence and relationships.*

Facts and truths may be learned by children, but faith is caught from those who are close to them. The relationship learning process implied in Deuteronomy 6:4–9 ('Impress them on your children. Talk about them when you sit at home and when you walk along the road, when you lie down and when you get up') is far more meaningful to a child than the formal teaching of words of wisdom. And it results in a faith-transfer, a flow-through of life truth, the catching of a good infection!

INTERGENERATIONAL WORSHIP

IGW is not a display of triviality that reduces worship to the level of a low-grade variety show. Traditional family services all too often descend to this level, with children being addressed as a species of sub-worshipper incapable of worshipping God with dignity in their own right. The result is overtones of entertainment for children and embarrassment for adults. (Family services, by the way, tend by the very title to disregard singles, teens, divorcees, widows and widowers, most of whom feel distinctly excluded.)

Nor is IGW a token attachment of children to an adult worship service, before being dispatched for 'their own programme'. It is something much richer and more meaningful than either of these.

General requirements for IGW

- *An intergenerational lifestyle in the church which facilitates natural interaction between children, teens, singles, divorced, middle-aged and elderly members.*

This implies broad-based communication, the learning of names, the sharing of interests and, above all, opportunities for experiencing meaningful relationships and fellowship right across the board.

- *Meaningful fellowship experiences into which people of all ages are carefully integrated, so that no-one is particularly conscious of any generational identification.*

As a result, each will be able to express with joy their thoughts, feelings and actions to God in whatever way is appropriate to them, and the entire congregation will function as a unity. In terms of John 4:24, IGW aims at creating lively worship activity in which the 'spirits' of both children and adults interact with the Spirit of God. If children are able to participate meaningfully in worship they will begin to feel allegiance to God. As a result, when the time comes for them to make a mature decision about their relationship to Christ, the choice facing them will be 'Will I leave the church, or not?', rather than, 'Will I join the church, or not?'

- *Contemporary, relevant and lively worship that includes and attracts all, particularly children and young people.*

If worship is a lively celebration, something enjoyable we do because of special occasions, and if children participate, it can become an attractive magnet, drawing non-worshippers without trauma into the worshipping company of God's people. A good news atmosphere of enjoyment and celebration, love and acceptance, will prove a strong attraction for an increasingly alienated world, and have a powerful evangelistic appeal. Many parents are seriously concerned about their children's moral welfare and, if included with their children in lively worship, might well be brought to faith themselves.

- *Worship experiences which teach, nurture and stimulate the faith of those who attend.*

Worshippers, at whatever stage they may be, are on a spiritual journey needing to be led through worship into the presence of God and into the next stage of their spiritual development.

The aims of IGW

- *To lead the whole congregation into a meaningful corporate worship experience.*

This calls for an environment in which all generations are together in worship, praising God, fellowshipping and learning together in an atmosphere conducive to the transference or transmission of faith.

- *To encourage each person, young or old, to participate meaningfully and relevantly in worship.*

This will be dependent on a sensitive awareness of the needs of each generation of worshippers represented, and a skilful ability to lead each into a warm encounter with God. The process will depend less on an addiction to words, explanations and teaching, and more on an ability to create a sense of wonder, and a pathway for each to find God for themselves.

- *To enable the congregation to experience a corporate expression of worship, so that each member, particularly the child, will enjoy a sense of belonging to the gathered people of God.*

In this atmosphere, relationships will develop and deepen into an accceptance of trust.

- *To maintain the basic identity of worship.*

James White writes in his book, *Intergenerational Religious Experience,* that although 'some of the elements of timing and form of worship services would be changed or at least affected by IG inclusiveness, the basic integrity of worship need not be compromised'. Essential to the biblical concept of worship is service. Servants and labourers expressed the worth of their master by bowing down and prostrating themselves before him. Early Christian worshippers expressed reverential fear, awe and wonder as they worshipped. Today's worship leader has the responsibility of leading worshippers into a service of 'worthship' or worship through a liturgy of praise, prayers, confession and the proclamation of God's word. However contemporary the service may be, the integrity of worship must be maintained. But if the worship leader's personality intrudes, cleverness will pervade the service, and entertainment will become the centrepiece. As a result, the 'wholeness' of worship will be impaired and broken, and with it its integrity. Because children have a genuine capacity for worship, and a strong perception of genuineness, there is no reason for violating the integrity of worship and allowing it to degenerate into triviality. Worship of the kind we are advocating is characterised by dignity, genuineness, wholeness and order, with attention being paid to language, pace, action, timeframes and so on.

Getting started

Probably the greatest resistance to any venture into IGW is summed up in the question, 'How do you get started?'

Vision for something different invariably comes from an individual, and nothing is likely to happen without one or more individuals who have carefully thought through the reasons for IGW and its implications, and who are convinced of the necessity for it to be introduced. They can initiate the creative process by beginning to talk to others about the need for real relationship between the generations throughout the church. This initial conviction will need to be channelled into a creative communication process, aimed at developing a wave of interest among the opinion-formers in the church.

No real progress can be expected until the leaders develop a genuine interest in and concern for IGW. Church leaders may be genuinely bewildered by the presence of children – possibly scared of them – and thus feel inadequate to handle them. Probably little or no reference was made in any training they may have received to the theology of childhood or ministry with children. They may be under extreme pressure already and feel unable to face extra demands in terms of time or preparation. Almost certainly, they will be anxious to avoid unnecessary conflict which is likely to arise from any tampering with worship tradition and practice.

The answer to this problem is a sensitive approach aimed at motivating and moving church leaders in the direction of accepting the theological and logical conclusions of IGW. When this is achieved, the congregation will need to be informed and educated about the leadership decision and the rationale behind the concept and practice of intergenerationalism. This will call for skilful communication which might comprise: addresses based on the theology of childhood; special studies for use in house group discussions; open seminars for the whole congregation.

A facilitating team will prove helpful, comprising people – hopefully of varying age – who are themselves willing to learn and who are committed to encouraging faith growth in the congregation through wholeness in the church's intergenerational life. Their tasks will be to direct the goals of the church towards an intergenerational lifestyle on as many levels as possible; to motivate the congregation to accept and work towards these goals; to feed in creative ideas and programmes to achieve the aims of IGW; to evaluate the success of IGW against self-set criteria; constantly to strive for better ways of achieving the goals; and to develop an ongoing self-education process which will give IGW a growing and developing profile in worship.

Guidelines for IGW

- *Careful planning is absolutely essential.*

If IGW services are to be successful they must be characterised by hard work, persistent prayer, creative thinking and careful structuring.

- *All-age involvement in planning is highly desirable.*

As well as helping to generate good ideas, it will give a greater diversity of people a sense of ownership in the service and also create greater momentum.

- *Be sensitive.*

Take into account the views of those who are resistant to change, and make a sincere attempt to accommodate them. As James White says, 'Our worship must be constructed around a healthy respect for the varieties of people who will be worshipping either in homogeneous or heterogeneous groups.'

- *Keep the service simple and short.*

Follow a single theme, and stick to it. Resist being complicated. Choose words and ideas within the range of children's comprehension, without becoming childish. (It is possible!) Keep the service short: 45 minutes is a useful guideline.

- *Adopt a liturgical framework.*

This requires not necessarily a repetitive procedure but a discernible order and structure. The worship service should not be thrown together in a haphazard way, but should contain the elements of worship – praise, confession, absolution, proclamation of God's word, and the worshippers' response.

- *Include meaningful and dignified involvement of people of all ages*

This will eliminate age consciousnesss, and prevent embarrassment for adults or superficial tokenism for children.

- *Avoid excessive talking.*

Overtalk, the delight of those adults who indulge in it, is a pain for children and adults alike.

- *Communicate.*

Make every aspect of the service as interesting as possible, so as to grip the attention of all. Stories well told, in the manner of Jesus, keep the congregation alert. Try to make the whole service communicate the message.

- *Keep the service lively and make the action and involvement continuous.*

Traditionally, most nonconformist churches have required the congregation to be passive recipients of the spoken word, apart from the welcome breaks for hymn singing. But the natural bent for

106

children is for movement, action, colour, imagination and involvement. In this visual and TV age, adults are not far behind! Stories, whether presented through telling, drama or mime, must actively attract the congregation into the story, so that they become part of it. Action and involvement can be enhanced by participation in welcoming people as they arrive, showing them to their seats, giving out books, taking up the offering, leading in prayer and reading the scriptures.

• *Make adequate technical arrangements.*

Those taking part need to be trained in whatever is required of them. Children, in particular, need to be helped to speak out, and the lectern and microphone need to be exactly the right height. Amplification is particularly important when children are participating, for nothing annoys crusty old-agers more than being unable to hear; and nothing annoys children more than being scorned for not doing their part properly.

• *Carefully select appropriate hymns and songs.*

These should convey the theme message of the service, contain understood words and ideas, and have enjoyable, lively, and singable tunes.

• *Carefully explain to participants what they are to do.*

This includes where to find the place in the Bible, where to sit, stand or kneel, and where the participant's contribution occurs in the service.

ONE MODEL OF INTERGENERATIONAL WORSHIP

One church decided to create a new service which would complement the traditional Sunday morning worship service and terminate the traditional Sunday school activity. Parents were approached regarding their responsibility for ministering to their children, and the possibility of creating a special IGW service which would support them in this. Approximately twenty pairs of parents agreed to act as family facilitators for groups which would include other families as well as their own children, interested relatives and friends of all ages. These units formed the basic structure of the new model which included the following elements.

- *Worshipping together*

This session brings together all age-groups, including pre-school children, for a period of worship which places special emphasis on singing, including new and older hymns and choruses. Open prayer, with children participating, is encouraged. The presence of pre-school children is acknowledged with a special song and a brief comment before they leave for their group work. This is conducted by appointed leaders, assisted by parents on a rota basis.

- *Teaching time*

Traditional sermons and children's talks are avoided, and a serious attempt is made to address all groups with dignity. This is achieved through the use of overhead transparencies, drama and any other creative way of presenting the message. Special efforts are made to communicate scripture through novel and creative ways, such as dramatised Bible reading.

The teaching has a two-fold aim: to project biblical concepts ('the telling of the story, as Jesus might have told it'), and the teaching of the message in deeper terms. The former occupies two-thirds of the teaching time; the latter tends to lose the younger children for a short while, but the service is designed to pick them up again in its next phase.

- *Discussion groups*

For these, the congregation is divided into two groups: teenagers and the majority of the adults; juniors and some of the parents. Although there is some separation of age-groups, everyone is together in the same place, and the dynamics of intergenerationalism are unaffected. Discussion material is provided for each group.

- *Take-home material*

This is provided for a two-fold purpose: to provide adults with some deeper teaching; and to provide teaching input for the family during the week.

- *Weekly peer-group activity*

It became evident that each age-group actually needed some peer-group activity, and so weeknight group activities were provided to fill this gap.

- *Quarterly communion*

This developed into a very special service in which all worship together until the pre-school children leave and the teaching is given. The younger children then return and communion takes the place of the discussion groups.

The overall principle holding the various aspects of worship together is that one integrated theme is presented which provides the same subject matter for all, though at different levels of understanding. The key questions are: have the children been acknowledged, included and catered for?; have the older people been challenged and involved in the learning process?

Evaluation

This model has been seen to present both positive features and negative problems.

Positive features

- The intergenerationalism of Psalm 78:1–8 has been given a platform on which to take place.

- Children have been included and have participated meaningfully with the people of God.

- Parents have been given the opportunity and have been helped to nurture their own children in the family of God.

- New leaders have emerged, and are enjoying the opportunity of serving God in this way. The 'Christian education staff' of the church has increased to a body of 40–60 adults, including many parents.

- The congregation as a whole has begun to demonstrate both care of and commitment to children, in this way creating a highly desirable intergenerational environment.

- The teaching content has improved, with the involvement of people of mature and demonstrated faith.

- Holiday church attendance, which previously had been fairly low, has picked up quite significantly.

- People have come to enjoy being at church, and seem to be in no hurry to go home.

- Younger couples have begun to identify with each other in the groups and are enjoying a greater degree of fellowship inside and outside of the church.

- A ministry of care and fellowship has developed among the 'family' groups, and has extended towards several church 'aunties, uncles and grandparents' who, in turn, have discovered a new dimension of happiness in their interaction with children.

- The value of faith-learning through relationships and example has been manifested.

Negative problems

- Difficulties have arisen in intergenerational face-to-face encounters within the groups. Some parents experience difficulty in discussing faith issues with their children, and even in discussing in any way with their teenagers. From the other side, teenagers admit to shyness in discussing faith matters with their parents and relatives. These symptoms appear to be a manifestation of the basic difficulties many families experience in communicating in-depth with their children.

Such difficulties are not regarded as insuperable, but as teething problems. If they can be overcome, an enormous positive influence will be released into both church and homes. If, however, they remain unsolved, the church will be faced once more with the problem of how to ensure the onflow of faith into the future.

- Teenagers battling to relate to an inter-age group confessed to feeling left out of the discussions, at times. This raises the possibility of an interim optional special group for teenagers alone.

However, a leader aware of this problem ought to be able to solve it with a sensitive approach to the teenagers in the group. Long-term, it is felt that children, having got used to communicating with adults, will project this attitude into adolescence, when their time comes.

- Some adults complained about the lack of intellectual depth in the presentations and discussions. The problem is acknowledged.

But is the sacrifice not worth making for the sake of the children, their faith, and their future in the church? And in any case, there are numerous opportunities for adult learning. The take-home material provides considerable food for thought; weekly Bible study groups exist for that very purpose; and the alternative adult-orientated Sunday morning service is available to supplement the intellectual deficiencies of the new model service.

- A number of so-called 'spiritual orphans' whose parents are unchurched but who had drifted into the Sunday school seem to have dropped off since the termination of traditional Sunday school activities.

It is felt, however, that, as the family spirit of the church develops and an emphasis is placed on winning the whole family, not only will the dropout be stemmed but the door will be opened for many more to be encouraged into the warm family environment of the church. What is more, the prospect of holding them will be greatly enhanced.

- The best problem to be faced is that some who have opted to attend the 10.00 am conventional service have indicated that they are missing the children. As a result, occasional morning services for everyone are being considered.

Questions for serious consideration

1. *What benefits do you imagine could arise from the implementation of an IGW service in your church?*
2. *What problems would you need to solve before considering implementing the kind of model suggested above?*
3. *If the above model seems inappropriate, what alternative model could you devise, if the burden of intergenerationalism rested upon you?*

7

Worship and life

Peter Cousins

*After a career in schooteaching and teacher training, Peter Cousins
went into publishing as Executive Director (editorial) for
Paternoster Press. A former editor of* Spectrum *and* Third Way,
he is the author of several books.

INTRODUCTION

In worship, extremes meet. For an example, consider this expression
of Anglo-Catholic spirituality:

> Wherefore, O Father, we thy humble servants
> Here bring before thee, Christ, thy well beloved,
> All-perfect offering, sacrifice immortal,
> Spotless oblation.

A twenty-year-old, brought up among the 'Brethren', found it easy
to identify with these sentiments. Again and again he had heard
the purpose of worship summed up in the formula, 'We are here
to give, not to receive.' This view could be expressed in a simple
diagram, showing worship moving along a vertical axis, from
below to above.

The same view of worship finds expression within the charismatic
movement. Here worship is often seen as a weapon in spiritual
warfare. As God is exalted by his people and given his rightful place,

battle is joined with the forces of evil, whose chief preoccupation is to deny God the high place which is due to him.

Such a view gives little attention to the concept of worship as involving a vertical movement from God to man. For example, where a service begins with the offertory – the placing of the bread and the wine upon the altar – the clear implication is that worship is something given by man to God. Even where there is no ritual expressing this thought, a formula such as: 'We are here to give, not to receive' expresses a similar attitude.

OLD TESTAMENT EVIDENCE

In his discussion of 'Mission and Worship' in the *Dictionary of Liturgy and Worship*,[1] J G Davies makes a similar point in a rather different way. He refers to the Old Testament understanding of Israel's vocation to be a holy people, and to express this holiness within their worship. Only thus can Israel become a 'light to the Gentiles'. In this connection,

> The function of worship . . . is to enable Israel to be holy; it is a means of sanctification for the Chosen People, who are set apart for the worship of Yahweh (Ex 19:6). The temple cultus is both the guarantee of the purity of Yahwism and the centre to which the nations are to come (Isa 2:2f). It will be noticed that Israel's vocation is interpreted centripetally; Israel is not sent to the nations; instead they are to come to it, attracted by its life and worship. In exact conformity with this, Israelite worship is similarly understood centripetally; it has its true centre in a single place, namely the Jerusalem temple, and it is to this that all the nations are to come.

A similar view is still influential today. Certainly it is true that in circles where a heavy emphasis is placed upon the concept of giving rather than receiving in worship, there has been considerable interest in Old Testament parallels. Once more, we may quote an Anglo-Catholic example.

_____

1. *SCM*, 1962.

And now O Father, mindful of the love
That bought us, once for all, on Calvary's tree,
And having with us him that pleads above,
We here present, we here spread forth to Thee,
That only offering perfect in Thy eyes,
The one true, pure, immortal sacrifice.

Elsewhere in the Christian church, not least among the 'Brethren', worship may be interpreted in terms of the various Levitical offerings. Such an understanding is undeniably faithful to one aspect of the Old Testament. Here, we find an elaborate system of sacrifices and offerings which are unquestionably to be offered *to* God by man. But closer study shows that these offerings themselves form part of a pattern ordained by God himself. The sacrifice of Noah is offered in response to God's saving act in deliverance from the Flood. In just the same way, the construction of the tabernacle and the revelation of a divine pattern for sacrifice, occur, not only after the deliverance from Egypt, but also after Israel's disobedience at Sinai and their worship of the golden bull. Here, the sacrificial system is seen as the gracious gift of God himself. The 'vertical' dimension of worship thus involves a double movement, from God to man in the first instance and from man to God in response.

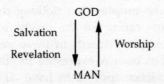

GOD

Salvation
Revelation

Worship

MAN

But the law was not concerned with the sacrificial system only. Israel's response to the saving love of God was to affect every detail of life: food, clothing, the family, agriculture – no aspect of human existence was untouched by the laws which were given by Yahweh, in love, when he revealed himself as Israel's saviour. Cultic activity in the temple and righteous living under the covenant were both equally a response to the gracious saving activity initiated by God himself. In Exodus 4:29–31, where God's people first hear the divine promises and learn that God is going to deliver them, they 'bow their heads in worship'. Worship is thus not only something offered by man to God, *but* also a response to what God offers to man. And it is expressed in a 'horizontal' dimension also, by the relationship of God's people to the world, to other believers, and to their fellow men and women.

It is not surprising that Israel tended to focus on the external, cultic aspects of worship. These were specific, limited and easily identified, and it was always possible for an Israelite to find satisfaction in having performed them. But the prophets consistently opposed this tendency. They repeatedly emphasized the importance for God's people of keeping *all* his commandments (Deut 5:29), not only those relating to the cultus. Samuel strikes a note which resounds throughout the Old and New Testament alike, when he affirms that God wants obedience rather than sacrifice (1 Sam 15:22) – an emphasis found also in Hosea (6:6) and on the lips of Jesus himself (Matt 9:13; 12:7). Such a response is unlimited. And who can claim success in loving his neighbour as himself.

Their concern for obedience within the covenant led the prophets to refer to worship divorced from obedience in terms which would be regarded as highly offensive today and, certainly, must have been so at the time when they spoke. Isaiah describes attending public worship as 'temple trampling' and says that God hates the cultus (Isa 1:1–17; cf Amos 5:21–24). Even more radical is Isaiah 58:1–7, where the practice of fasting is drastically reinterpreted. Here the specifically religious activity is emphatically displaced. True fasting, says the prophet, has nothing to do with religious observance. It means caring for the needy, and liberating poor people who are being oppressed. In these verses the 'religious' activity of fasting has been re-expressed in ethical terms and the vertical Godward aspect appears to have all but vanished in a process that has been described as 'desacralization'. Similarly, Jeremiah desacralizes circumcision (Jer 9:25f). Paul makes the same point in Romans 2:29. In the same way, Jeremiah 22:16 identifies 'knowing God' with ensuring that fair treatment is given to the poor and needy.

Even sacrificial worship is subjected to this desacralizing process. In New Testament times, the writer to the Hebrews saw clearly that animal sacrifices could never atone for sin, even though they had been divinely ordained (10:1–4). The reason why the self-offering of Christ could achieve what the blood of bulls and goats was powerless to bring about was that Christ surrendered his will to the service of God (10:7–9), which they could never do. It was in this way that Christ fulfilled the inadequate cultus of the Old Testament.

But the Old Testament sacrificial system had been recognized as inadequate even by worshippers who identified with it.

> The sacrifices of God are a broken spirit
> A broken and a contrite heart,
> O God thou wilt not despise.
> (Psa 51:17).

Here is desacralization of an extreme kind. When a sinner stands face to face with God, there is nothing to be achieved by offering sacrifice. Indeed, God is not really interested in receiving it. The only appropriate response is a personal one, coming from deep within the worshipper himself, expressed in personal repentance and, by implication, in the obedience which flows from repentance.

But, in spite of the prophetic tradition which seems to devalue the cultus and to re-express such activities as fasting and Sabbath keeping in terms of love to the neighbour, the 'vertical' element in worship has not totally disappeared. In what Isaiah 58 says about fasting, in the reinterpretation of circumcision offered by Jeremiah and Paul, and in the moving cry of Psalm 51, we find a realization that individuals can offer God their penitence, their self-mortification, and their deeds of love – in worship.

A response of this kind took on new significance after the destruction of Jerusalem by the Babylonians. Jews who were exiled from Jerusalem were no longer able to offer sacrifices in the place and manner that God had appointed. But the worship of individual response and obedience was still possible, and centuries later Jesus himself sanctioned it when he spoke of both prayer and almsgiving as being directed toward 'your Father in heaven' (Matt 6:4–6).

Synagogue worship was, indeed, largely desacralized. The rabbi had no cultic role. The only sacred object in the synagogue was the scroll of the law, to obey which was to worship God. Yet even in this context, religiosity and perverted devotion intruded. Jesus found it necessary to rebuke worshippers who scrupulously gave tithes of herbs but were unjust, unloving and dishonest in daily life (Matt 23:23). He condemned some who even used their religion as a pretext for disobeying the sixth commandment (Mark 7:9–12). Clearly, Jesus took his place within the Old Testament prophetic tradition. Indeed, to him, the horizontal relationship was ultimately more important than the vertical. At the most sacred moment of all, he said, when the worshipper was about to place his gift on the altar of God, he was to quit the temple, leaving his gift behind him, rather than remain unreconciled to his fellow-Israelite (Matt 5: 23–24).

The implication is clear. Jesus is again reinforcing the message of Hosea. God has made the downward movement of self-revelation. The response of the worshipper is to be expressed horizontally, as well as vertically, upwards. And the horizontal takes precedence. 'I desire mercy, not sacrifice.'

Micah 6:6–8 explicitly answers the question of what God requires from the worshipper. The prophet denies that God is interested in offerings of animals – let alone of children. What he seeks from true worshippers is expressed in words which have rich Old Testament associations. They are 'justice' and 'mercy', both of which clearly relate to relationship with other men and women. To 'walk humbly with God' implies adopting a certain way of life ('walk') which is to be characterized by 'humble submission to God'.

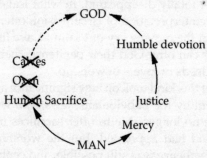

NEW TESTAMENT EVIDENCE

It would be easy to write at length about the forms of worship under the old covenant. But when we turn to the New Testament, directions about worship are conspicuous by their absence. Certainly Christians are obligated to baptize and to share a symbolic meal of bread and wine. The New Testament also makes it clear that the first Christians prayed together, sang, spoke in tongues, taught and exhorted each other and prophesied. These activities are referred to in Luke's chronicle of the Acts of the Holy Spirit. But most of what we know about Christian worship is gleaned from the correspondence of Paul, a church-planter, who wrote at length about the subject because he was concerned to correct abuses that had become widespread in one congregation, at Corinth. (Possibly two congregations, if those interpreters are correct who think that in the background to 1 Timothy we can glimpse the gnosticizing and liberated women of Ephesus.)

This is a remarkable state of affairs and for many Christians a disquieting one. Even during the decades following the completion of the New Testament, church leaders did what they could to establish rules for the conduct of Christian worship. But such attempts are foreign to the spirit of the New Testament itself. Equally alien are more recent efforts emanating from Rome, Wittenberg, Geneva, and Plymouth. An unbiased reading of the canonical documents of the Christian faith will lead us to conclude, with dismay or delight, that God is really not very interested in the externals of worship. In this connection, it is surely significant that when the Samaritan woman asked Jesus where worship should be conducted, she was told that the place was irrelevant ('neither in Jerusalem nor on Mount Gerizim') but that the one essential was that it should be 'in spirit and truth'.

All the same, there is a measure of continuity between the old covenant and the new. It is found in the typically biblical concern shown for the lifestyle of the worshippers. How is it possible, Paul asks, for someone who has been baptized and incorporated into the body of Christ, to unite the members of Christ with those of a prostitute (1 Cor 6:15)? He warns his hearers that baptism and a place at the Lord's table will not in themselves act as a safeguard against disasters such as overtook God's people of the old covenant when they disobeyed him (1 Cor 10:1–14). The Holy Spirit did not lead Paul to give any instructions about who was to preside at the Lord's Supper, or what words are to be spoken over the bread and wine. Instead, we are left with the solemn warning that we profane the ordinance if we are guilty of loveless behaviour to fellow members of Christ's body (1 Cor 11:18, 21, 29).

As for baptism, not only does the New Testament give no detailed instructions about how this is to be carried out, but Paul shows remarkably little concern about whether or not he had personally baptized anybody at all at Corinth (1 Cor 1:13–17).

In addition to this lack of detailed instruction about the ordinances of the new covenant, the New Testament shows little concern about the assortment of behaviours and emotions that we commonly refer to as worship. We can scarcely doubt that members of the early communities experienced awe, adoration, penitence, joy and other emotions associated with worship, when they met together. But, as Howard Marshall has pointed out in a challenging article,[1] the New Testament rarely portrays the church as engaging in what we have come to think of as typically 'worship' activity. It may be a good thing to conduct a solemn eucharist, whether this ends with the notices for the coming week or with *Ite, missa est*, or to listen to a protracted sermon, or to enjoy a celebration of charismatic praise – but we shall find none of these prescribed or even described in the New Testament.

So what guidance does the New Testament give us about the motifs underlying worship? In the first instance, we shall look at the distinctively Christian observance of the Lord's Supper. Second, we shall examine the New Testament use of some words which have special significance for the activity of worship.

Lord's Supper

For many Christians, the Lord's Supper provides above all an opportunity for individual communion with the Lord.

> Here, O my Lord, I see thee face to face . . .

The daily concerns of suffering and sinful humanity are to be shut out.

> Here from the world we turn,
> Jesus to seek . . .

Even where there is an emphasis upon fellowship it excludes those who are not believers:

---

1. *Churchman*, 99:3, 1985, 216–219.

Shut in with thee, far far above
The restless world that wars below . . .

Admittedly such an understanding may lead to the Lord's Supper
being perceived as a means of gaining strength for service in the
world. There is a beautiful communion hymn based on the Liturgy
of Malabar which sounds this note:

Strengthen for service, Lord, the hands
That holy things have taken.

But to stop at this point is to come short of acknowledging the very
close link which is apparent between the ordinance of the Lord's
Supper and everyday life. The bread and wine themselves, for
example, speak of daily reality. More precisely, perhaps, we should
say that they will have done so in their original life setting. Unfor-
tunately, port-style wine has its own rather different connotations
in Western cultures, and the use of elaborate goblets and platters
further distances the event from normal experience. Even so, a loaf
of ordinary leavened bread is adequate to evoke that flesh which
Jesus said his disciples must chew (John 6:53–56, Greek). In the
Lord's Supper, we celebrate a saviour who became flesh, and in
biblical terms it is precisely 'flesh' which unites us all in the bundle
of life. 'All flesh', is the biblical term for humankind, even for the
whole world of living beings (Gen 7:21–22). Nothing could be more
'down to earth' than the incarnation, or the sacrament that symbol-
izes it.

One loaf, one body – when they give each other the peace during
the Eucharist, Christians affirm the basically horizontal thrust of the
supper, and this, as we have seen, is prominent in Paul's teaching
about the Breaking of Bread. Indeed, he repeatedly emphasizes in
what he says about worship, that everything done when the community meets together must be tested by whether it builds up the
body. Intense spiritual experience accompanying tongues-speaking
is disvalued in this context – Christians do not meet together with a
view to individual self-edification. Mutual concern one for another
is to be the hallmark of Christian worship as of Christian living
(1 Cor 14: 3–5, 17).

The cup saying is explicitly linked to the forgiveness of sins. No
doubt the self-offering of Jesus on the cross was an act of obedience

to the father, fulfilling the burnt-offering element in the Old Testament cultus, but at the Lord's Supper we are reminded, not of this, but of the fact that his blood was shed in order to secure forgiveness for sinful men and women. In view of this, it is difficult to argue, as some have done, that 'worship is more important than evangelism'.

It is doubtful whether there should ever be a celebration of the supper without a prayer for the preaching of the gospel which it portrays so powerfully.

Not only is the Saviour's blood covenant blood, 'shed for the forgiveness of sins'. It is also offered to the worshippers with the injunction: 'Drink of it, all of you'. The most basic imperative of the gospel of forgiveness is a horizontal one. How can Christians look up to heaven and give thanks for the forgiveness of their sins while refusing to look around at the brothers and sisters (even their own husbands or wives) whom they are unwilling to forgive for the sin – real or imaginery – that they have committed against them?

'God so loved the world that he gave...' Some religious traditions seek to shut the world out of the upper room, but the bread and the wine will not be silenced. Christ's people, confronted by the symbols of God's love for a ruined world, must inevitably think of its anguish and desperate need. After all, to take the elements in Christ's name means that we commit ourselves to the mission that motivated the Son of God, the Divine Image, to take the form of a servant, and led him first to Bethlehem and then to Calvary. The word sacrament was used of a Roman soldier's oath of allegiance, and when we reaffirm our new covenant commitment to the Lord Jesus, we commit ourselves also to a life of service, self-giving, and sacrificial peacemaking.

This theology of the cross leads – or drives – us into the world. It is a false theology of glory that focuses exclusively on personal communion with the ascended Christ. Ben Patterson, a Presbyterian minister in Orange County, California, comments: 'Historically the more Christians focus on *experiencing* the presence of God, the less interested they are in the poor and the hungry.' He continues, referring to the prosperity-orientated charismatic spirituality that is fashionable today: 'People in these new churches are experiencing all these wonderful things and they are into diet and health and prosperity, but there is no concern for justice'. Amos and Isaiah would have recognized the symptoms of a disease which blights the worship of 'Brethren', Catholic and Charismatic alike.

This reluctance to relate the experience of worship to human need is remarkable, in view of the way that the circumstances of the Saviour's death evoke human suffering. Doublecrossed by his friend, rejected by his own people, a political prisoner subjected to dubious judicial proceedings, weakened by torture, stripped naked, hungry and thirsty, dying a solitary death, the person of the crucified Christ brings before worshippers the plight of millions in the world today. But human suffering in the world today is not the whole story.

The Lord's Supper is intended to help us focus on a glorious future, when we will drink with the Lord in the kingdom (Luke 22:18). A right interpretation of the New Testament sees this kingdom as already present wherever Jesus is acknowledged as Lord, although its full manifestation is not yet. We are the children of the kingdom, pledged to the life of the new age and living out its hope, its challenge and its compassion for the poor. For some Christians, however, 'my Father's Kingdom' refers to a heavenly realm having no connection with what happens on earth.

A defective theology has too often been responsible for excluding from the Lord's Supper any thought of our suffering world. Wherever Christians believe that heaven is for the church and the earth is for Israel, they will be in danger of closing their eyes to human need and of turning away from the kingdom challenge of the Lord's Supper. As we have already noted, the New Testament contains little detailed information about Christian worship. This apparent indifference to times, places and rituals is not surprising in view of our Lord's attitude. In the words of J S McEwen:[1]

> The principle laid down by Jesus is that of the complete relativity of the external form of worship. *Any* form or rule is good which is proved by experience to be an aid to that worship which is in spirit and in truth. A further consequence of Jesus' teaching is that the barrier between sacred and secular, worship and daily living, crumbles away. Since worship means the service of God, and this in turn implies loving one's neighbour, it follows that every kindly act performed in this spirit and intention is an act of worship (Matt 25:34–40; Jas 1:27).

---

1. *Wittenberg Door*, No 19, p 18.

New Testament words

What McEwen says about the disappearance of the barrier between sacred and secular, worship and daily living certainly corresponds to what we find in Paul. The implications of Romans 12:1, for example, are immense. At this point in the epistle, Paul has ended his account of God's saving purposes for the world and for Israel with a doxology expressing awe and worship (11: 33–36). Now he demands a response from his hearers: they must surrender their lives to the God who has saved them. The word he uses, however, is not 'lives', but 'bodies' and he goes on to describe such self-surrender as a living sacrifice, their 'spiritual worship' (RSV). 'The language throughout this clause', writes C K Barrett,[1] 'is sacrificial; not only the word "sacrifice" itself, but also "offer", "holy", and "well-pleasing" are technical terms.' Nor is this the only occasion when the New Testament describes the actions of Christians in terms of sacrifice. The faith of the Philippians is a sacrifice (Phil 2:17); so is the gift they sent to Paul (Phil 4:18); doing good to others (Heb 13:16); praise (Heb 13:15); all may perhaps be included in the 'spiritual sacrifices' of 1 Peter 2:5.

In 1 Peter 2:5, Peter speaks of the offerings made by the church, but does not specify precisely what are the 'spiritual sacrifices' which the holy Christian priesthood should bring. In a very helpful contribution to a volume edited by D Carson, *The Church in the Bible and the World*, (Paternoster, 1987), Russell P Shedd quotes L Goppelt: 'They are not physically acts that are carried out in obedience to the letter, but Spirit-inspired surrender to all kinds of service.'

The self-offering enjoined upon Christians in Romans 12:1 is described as a *logiken latreian*. Originally used of hired service, *latreia* and the associated verb *latreuo* are used in the New Testament of worshipping God. The best interpretation of *logikos* here is probably that of Cranfield, who sees the word as implying a response based on a right understanding of the gospel and salvation.

All the same, it is apparent that Paul did not intend to reduce Christian worship to life in the Spirit, rejecting all external forms. Recognising this leaves us with the question of whether the language of Romans 12:1 may not simply be figurative. After all, even today, in a world where religious sacrifice is largely a thing of the past, we

---

1. *The Epistle to the Romans*, A & C Black, 1957.

still use the term metaphorically. 'It was a real sacrifice', we say, 'when Jane gave up a summer holiday to care for a sick neighbour.' In such a context, the term has no religious significance for us. Did it have such a significance for Paul?

There are two reasons for thinking that it had. One is that Paul lived in a world where sacrifice was very much a physical and literal reality. In this setting, to say that money sent to him for Christ's sake or good deeds by Christians were sacrifices was more than metaphor. His use of cultic imagery (see the quotation from C K Barrett above) reinforces this conclusion. So does the use of the word *latreia*, as may be seen from its occurrence in Romans 9:4; Hebrews 9:1. Paul seems to have believed that, for the Christian, worship and life are not separate entities, related to each other less or more closely. He stands in the Old Testament prophetic tradition reaffirmed by Jesus, asserting that, for God's people, life and worship must be *coterminous*. Horatius Bonar had the same vision when he sought:

> Praise in the common things of life,
>   Its goings out and in;
> Praise in each duty and each deed,
>   However small and mean . . .
> So shall no hour of day or night
>   From sacredness be free;
> But all my life, in every step,
>   Be fellowship with thee.

Shedd sees the traditional lists of admonitions to wives, husbands, children, parents and slaves, so often found in Paul's letters, as

> a remarkable illustration . . . of what Paul meant by the sacrifice of the whole of life to God. Christians in bondage are urged not to offer 'eyeservice' to please their masters. On the contrary they must consider themselves as slaves of Christ, serving him "with sincerity of heart, fearing the Lord" (Col 3:22; cf Eph 6:5–7). This language borders on the cultic. All Christians are encouraged to sing in their hearts to God (Eph 5:19; Col 3:16). Slaves are to work heartily, as if they were offering their service as a sacrifice to the Lord (rather than begrudging their unpaid labour). Though these sacrifices of body, praise and good deeds may seem remarkably

125

mundane, they are well-pleasing to God. Extraordinary acts of piety, through self-affliction or ascetic abstinence, are not encouraged (Col 2: 16–23). What counts is love of God and neighbours. Without such genuine love, self-immolation is quite worthless (1 Cor 13:3).

If we are justified in understanding Romans 12:1 as being more than a 'mere' metaphor, we may also cite other places where Paul seems to apply the language of worship to activities which are in no way concerned with cultic activity. In Philippians 2:17, Paul's death is regarded as a *drink-offering*, to be poured out upon the *sacrifice* of the Philippians' faith. In Philippians 2:25, Epaphras was the *minister* who by bringing their gifts to Paul, provided him with a *ministry* which they could not supply. In 2 Corinthians 9:12 gifts for the poor of Jerusalem are a *service*, and in Romans 15:16 proclaiming the good news is a *priestly duty* (NIV). In several cases the word used is one of the forms of *leitourgeo*. Although the noun can be used of secular rulers who do not act consciously as servants of God, yet discharge their functions which are an ordinance of God (Rom 13:6), the word has powerful associations with worship. We may cite Hebrews 10:11, referring to the service of priests and Levites under the law, and also Acts 13:2, where it is used of the period of prayer and worship by the church leaders at Antioch preceding the setting aside of Saul and Barnabas.

CONCLUSION

When we look at Christian sacrifice and the universal priesthood of the church from the viewpoint of the New Testament, it is clear that these have become integral aspects of any Christian definition of worship. 'Like a flowing spring', writes Shedd, 'a continuously renewed fellowship with him who sacrificed himself unreservedly for the church ought to motivate all who worship to bring God's saving solution to the world's desperate need.' He quotes H Berkhof, who speaks of worship as:

an antiphonal event in which, to the one side, God comes to us in such elements as proclamation of grace, command, Scripture reading, preaching, meal, and benediction; and in which, to the other side, we come before God with our confession of sin, litany of praise, profession of faith, prayers and intercessions, gifts for his work in the church and in the world, and hymns of humiliation and adoration, of praise and petition.

Shedd comments that 'such familiar exercises in worship are not worthy of him who lived his *whole* life for us, unless the members voluntarily choose to respond attitudinally in a manner that moves them joyfully to offer *all* of their actions and service on the altar of sacrifice'. The closing paragraphs of Shedd's study, which came to my attention only after I had begun work on this essay, express very clearly what the Bible has to say about the relationship between worship and life.

> The average congregation, with its facile, traditional approach to worship, sees a duty to perform in the acting out of the liturgy as though that were the sum of the *leitourgia* (priestly service) the New Testament priesthood is invited to bring to God. Once the hour of service has ended the Christian feels free to sink back into the neutral ('secular') routine of daily living in the world. I have no desire to denigrate the significance of repeated worship services, but the New Testament surely challenges us all to recapture the totality of its conception of worship. All thoughts, words and deeds should be performed as worship because the Lamb is 'worthy to receive power and wealth and wisdom and strength and honour and glory and blessing' (Rev 5:12). The sevenfold offering, which the innumerable angelic hosts proclaim the slain Lamb is worthy to receive, can be given in reality only by the redeemed on earth. For his honour, glory and blessing, we speak, write, work, play, eat and sleep, for he is worthy of all of the life power that pulsates within us.
>
> The public gatherings of the church ought to have this objective in constant view. Her members should be stimulated, even as they participate in the liturgy, to practice actions of love and good deeds (Heb 10:24). Together or scattered, the church should be a glorifying community. Only such two-faceted worship is worthy of him who gave himself for the church with the intention of securing her perfection (Eph 5:27). For we are not our own, but have been bought with a price (1 Cor 6:20), meaning that Chris-

tians have as much free time as slaves! 'Therefore whether you eat or drink or whatever you do, do everything for the glory of God' (1 Cor 10:31).

For Further Reading

Biblical

Brown, C (ed), *The New International Dictionary of New Testament Theology*, Paternoster, 1975–8, articles on: 'Prayer. . . worship' (II.855–866); 'Serve. . . worship' (III.544–553).

Martin, R P, *Worship in the Early Church*, Eerdmans, 1974.

Peterson, D, *Engaging with God*, Apollos, 1992.

Van Gemeren, W A, *New International Dictionary of Old Testament Theology*, Paternoster, 1997, article on 'hwh' (2556), (II. 42–44.)

General

Beasley-Murray, P, *Faith and Festivity*, Monarch, 1991.

Carson, D A (ed), *Worship: Adoration and Action*, Paternoster, 1993.

Carson, H, *Hallelujah! Christian Worship*, Evangelical Press, 1980.

Davies, J G (ed), *A New Dictionary of Liturgy and Worship*, SCM Press, 1986.

Kendall, RT, *Worshipping God*, Hodder & Stoughton, 1989. (Reprinted, Paternoster, 1997).

Kendrick, G, *Worship*, Kingsway, 1984.

Tozer, AW, *Whatever Happened to Worship?*, Kingsway/OM Publishing, 1986.

John Baigent

About Partnership

A fellowship of individuals and churches (mainly with Brethren roots), Partnership's main aim is to encourage the application of biblical principles to the changing conditions of modern life, particularly in the area of church life and witness.

Partnership publishes a magazine, *Partnership Perspectives*, three times a year; a broadsheet, *Partnership Update*, twice a year; and an *International Newsletter* once a year. It publishes several books, booklets and study guides each year.

Enquiries regarding individual and church subscriptions should be directed to the executive secretary, Dr Neil Summerton, 52 Hornsey Lane, London N5 6LU (Tel: 0171 272 0643).

Partnership publications may be obtained from Paternoster Press, PO Box 300, Carlisle, Cumbria, CA3 0QS (Tel: 01228 512 512; Fax: 01228-514949; Web:http://paternoster-publishing.com)

A full listing of Partnership Publications appears below:

Editor: Peter Brierley

The Christian Brethren as the Nineties Began

The results of a 1988 survey of independent congregations in the British Isles set alongside the relevant statistics of the 1989 English church census present not only useful information on the current state of the Brethren Movement, but also indications as to future developments.

0-900128-09-7 / pb / iv+112pp / 229 × 145 mm / £6.99

Neil Dickson

Modern Prophetesses

Women Preachers in the Nineteenth-Century Scottish Brethren *(Partnership Booklets)*

0-900128-14-3 / pb / 28pp / 210 × 145 mm / £1.50

Kevin G. Dyer

Must Brethren Churches Die?

After an introductory chapter by John Allan, the author analyses four factors which must characterize healthy churches—unity, leadership, change and vision—and asks the question: What must be done to rekindle the flame which is in danger of going out?

0-900128-08-9 / pb / 79pp / 210 × 145 mm / £4.99

Jonathan Lamb

Making Progress in Church Life
How to Handle Change Positively

The author writes in his Introduction, 'Wise Christian leadership seems to me to be a marriage of the pastoral and the strategic. By this I mean it is vitally important to set biblical priorities and direction for our churches, but this is to be done in the context of a care for each member of the congregation. The pastoral metaphor of the shepherd, so familiar to the biblical writers, contains elements of both leadership and care which are specially needed in handling change positively'.

0-900128-17-8 / stitched / 48pp / 210 × 148 mm / £3.50

Cedric Longville

Go Tell My Brothers—
Christian Women and Church Worship

It is commonly held that the apostle Paul ruled against women speaking publicly in church worship. The author here sizes up the traditional arguments for this position against the biblical material pertinent to the question, starting with the accounts of the first witnesses of the risen Christ. His conclusion, a challenge to rethink widely-held views, seeks to do justice to Christ's status as sole head of his worshipping people. Cedric Longville is a Christian lawyer living in Cardiff.

0-900128-13-5 / pb / xiv + 142pp / 229 × 145 mm / £7.99

Henry Ratter

Buried Talents

Or, *God Given Gifts for Building His Church*

The author, a chemical engineer working with ICI, has been involved in numerous roles, including the leadership of business teams and human resource development. In this brief book he brings his experience to bear on the problem of developing individual talent in the local church. Valuable Appendixes include *Job Profiles*, *Analysing Your Gift*, *Training Materials* and *Work Analysis*. A highly practical, biblically based little manual.

0-900128-18-6 / stitched / 71pp / 210 × 148 mm / £4.99

Olive Rogers, Sally Hogg et al

Does God Expect Less of Women?

Until recently the church certainly did 'expect less' of women than it did of men. There is a good deal of evidence that some Christians still do. This series of Bible studies goes beyond details of practice to investigate biblical principles.

0-900128-15-1 / pb / 32pp / 210 × 148mm / £2.99

D D Ronco

Risorgimento and the Free Italian Churches, now Churches of the Brethren

A fascinating historical study from an expert in the field.
(Available from: Dr D D Ronco, 1 Hendyrpeg, Penmyndd Road, Menai Bridge, Gwynedd LL 59 5RU).

Editor: Harold H. Rowdon

The Brethren Contribution to the Worldwide Mission of the Church

This collection of papers is a record of the International Brethren Conference on Missions held at the Anglo-Chinese School in Singapore. Issues covered are biblical and theological, historical, ideological, and practical.

0-900128-12-7 / pb / 127pp / 229 × 145mm / £5.99

Editor: Harold H. Rowdon

Churches in Partnership for Strengthening and Growth

A follow-up to the Nantwich Consultation, these are the edited papers of a consultation held at the University of Warwick. Themes covered include inter-church co-operation, the training of leaders, and openness to other traditions.

0-900128-11-9 / pb / 80pp / 229 × 145mm / £4.99

Editor: Harold H Rowdon

Declare His Glory
Congregational Worship Today

Fifteen years ago, *Partnership* recognised the urgent need for biblical reflection and practical advice on the subject of worship, and published the first edition of *Declare His Glory*.

This new edition is a major development of the original, with a new Introduction by Jonathan Lamb, a completely new chapter on worship and the Lord's Supper, and revised and much-expanded material on the practice of worship today. John Baigent's thorough biblical foundation for worship remains, as does John Allan's brilliant treatment of music, movement and silence in worship, and Peter Cousins' reflections on worship and life.

0-900128-20-8 / pb / 144pp / 216 × 135 mm / £8.99

Editor: Harold H Rowdon

Don't Muzzle the Ox

Full-time Ministry in Local Churches

This book provides valuable guidance for churches planning to appoint full-time workers. Biblical principles are clearly spelled out, whilst matters relating to selection and appointment are dealt with in detail.

The book moves on to examine working relationships with other local church leaders, the full-time worker's spirituality and effective use of time.

Though written primarily for churches with a Brethren background, *Don't Muzzle the Ox* contains material, much of it not readily available elsewhere, useful for any church seeking full-time help.

0-9001280-19-4 | pb | 108pp | 229 × 145 mm | £4.99

Editor: Harold H. Rowdon

The Strengthening, Growth and Planting of Local Churches

Papers on key issues facing independent congregations, such as leadership, youth work, women in the church, church-planting models, and race, class and social character.

0-900128-10-0 | pb | 141pp | 210 × 145mm | £6.99

Neil W Summerton

Local Churches for a New Century

A Strategic Challenge

After describing briefly the present situation in Brethren churches and its origins, the author present readers with a series of strategic pointers for the next century, challenging them with fresh insights on subjects as diverse as spirituality, cultural relevance, worship, pastoral care, the role of women and effective communication.

0-900128-16-X | stitched | 23pp | 216 × 148 mm | £2.50

Neil Summerton

A Noble Task

Eldership and Ministry in the Local Church (Revised Edition)

'I would urge everyone involved with local church leadership and developments in local ministry to read A Noble Task—for its inspiration, practical common sense, and balanced biblical analysis of important ministry issues.'—Churchman

0-85364-515-9 / pb / 213pp / 216 × 135mm / £9.99

Christian Brethren Review Backlist

41. *Scottish Brethren 1838–1916 and other papers.* (£4.00)

40. *Into all the world. Papers on world mission today: understanding it, practising it, teaching it.* (£4.50)

39. *Declare His glory: A fresh look at our congregational worship.* (First edition) (£4.00)

38. *Handling differences: How to disagree without disintegrating.* (£2.00)

37. *Servants of God: Papers on the use of full-time workers in Brethren churches.* (First edition, 1986) (£3.50)

36. *World Mission Today: The challenge of mission today, its biblical basis, training, accountability.* (£3.50)

35. *The Caring Church: Papers on counselling and pastoral care.* (£3.50)

31–32. *The Bible in the Eighties.* (£3.50)

29. *Neo-Pentecostalism/Urban Evangelism.* (£1.50)

28. *The Biblical doctrine of man/John Synge and the early Brethren.* (£1.00)

27. *Sex Ethics.* (£1.50)

Brethren Archivists and Historians Network Review

Vol. 1, No. 1, Autumn 1997 (£5.00)

Membership of the Brethren Archivists and Historians Network is open for an annual subscription of £UK10 to residents of the British Isles and £16 (at the particular rate of exchange prevailing at any time) for those located elsewhere. Applications and subscriptions should be sent to Neil Dickson, 6 Belleisle Place, Kilmarnock, Ayrshire KA1 4 UD, UK.

Occasional papers (new series)

Peter Brierley, *Growing churches at the July 1993 Warwick Consultation*. (1.00, p & p inc.) *Available from the Executive Chairman of Partnership, Dr Neil Summerton, 52 Hornsey Lane, London N6 5LU.*

Publications Archive Listing

A hand list of all Christian Brethren Research Fellowship and Partnership publications since 1963 is available from the Executive Chairman of Partnership, Dr Neil Summerton, 52 Hornsey Lane, London N6 5LU—who will also be pleased to receive membership subscriptions (£20 per annum for individuals; and 80p per annum per member for corporate subscription by local churches (subject to a minimum payment of £30 for churches of 38 members/regular attenders or less, and a maximum of £90 for churches with more than 112 members/regular attenders)).

Library Deposits

CBRF and Partnership publications are deposited with the British Library, the National Library of Wales and the National Library of Scotland, and can also be seen at the Christian Brethren Archive of the John Rylands University Library, University of Manchester, Oxford Road, Manchester M13 9PP (contact David Brady). Dr Brady is happy to be contacted about access to items which are out of print, and also about access to the manuscript collections included in the Archive.

Tapes

Tapes of addresses given at CBRF and Partnership national seminars and consultations are available from D J Scott, 40 Bakewell Road, Hazel Grove, Stockport, SK7 6JU (price £1.50 per item, plus £0.50p per order postage and packing). A list of tapes is available from him or from the Executive Secretary.

Back Copy Availability

Subject to availability, back copies of Partnership Newsletters (New Series) and *Partnership Perspectives* (the magazine which has replaced the new series of newsletters) can be obtained from the Executive Secretary, price £1.25 per item (+ £0.25p postage and packing).